ON TO THE
SUNSET

ON TO THE SUNSET

THE LIFETIME ADVENTURES OF A SPIRITED PIONEER

Ethel Burnett Tibbits

FIFTH
HOUSE

Fifth House edition published 2002.

Design by Articulate Eye

Front cover photograph by Daryl Benson / Masterfile

The publisher gratefully acknowledges the support of The Canada Council for the Arts and the Department of Canadian Heritage. We acknowledge the financial support of the Government of Canada through the Book Publishing Industry Development Program for our publishing activities.

Printed in Canada by Transcontinental Printers

02 03 04 05 06 / 5 4 3 2 1

National Library of Canada Cataloguing in Publication Data

Tibbits, Ethel Burnett.

On to the sunset

ISBN 1-894004-86-8

1. McCarty, Albert. 2. Pioneers—Canada, Western—Biography.
3. Frontier and pioneer life—Canada, Western. I. Title.
FC541.M22T52 2002   971.2'02'092   C2002-910355-X
F1060.9.M32T52 2002

Fifth House Ltd.
A Fitzhenry & Whiteside Company
1511-1800 4 St. SW
Calgary, Alberta, Canada
T2S 2S5

1-800-387-9776
www.fitzhenry.ca

THIS BOOK IS DEDICATED TO THE GRANDCHILDREN, WHO WILL BE GRATEFUL THAT THESE TALES OF A PIONEER GRANDFATHER HAVE BEEN PRESERVED, A PIONEER WHO, WITH HIS FAMILY, MOVED EVER WESTWARD ACROSS DEVELOPING CANADA UNTIL HE REACHED THE SUNSET.

CONTENTS

CHAPTER I

The Young Irish Stowaway

These are the stories that were told by Albert McCarty, the Pioneer, as he sat in the home of his daughter, Margo McCarty Maxwell out on the Pacific Coast during those last, long months of his life—stories Margo was to preserve as a permanent record of early Canadian living, as well as a tribute to a worthy and colourful Canadian, her father.

Sitting in his deep chesterfield chair day after day, as the old heart slowly faded into a tired pianissimo, always expectant of a return of strength despite his four-score years and seven, the Pioneer delighted to let his mind travel back over the long trail whence he had come, and paint pictures of his colourful past as they sprang continuously to his clear mind. Peoples, places, experiences—all came vividly from the pages of memory's book, and he found in his younger daughter, Margo, an ever-ready and appreciative audience.

While his eighty-seven years had been typical of those lived by the thousands of pioneers who faced toil and privation in those raw years of the century which was theirs, it is contended that few came through such successive defeats and failures, as well as triumphs and achievements, with head held higher than did this six-foot-two narrator of these tales of early Canada.

This was, perhaps, because of his Irish ancestry. Albert's father, old James McCarty, had become a Canadian citizen only by reason of his refusal to be excluded. Because there was no other way, he waited until the ship had just moved from the dock, when he made a rush for the gangplank (already swinging in mid-air) and got aboard. At the age of twelve, he landed in Canada as a stowaway, and what he had to overcome before he had wrested something like a living from the forbidding Ontario backwoods must have been a constant inspiration to his long son Albert.

It was in the year 1832 that James Hill McCarty migrated to America, and that was a time of desperate poverty in Ireland. Conditions became so acute that a plan was worked out in the various parishes whereby wealthy landowners contributed funds to send emigrants to the new world. Grandfather McCarty was beneficiary to none of that assistance, although no boy in Ireland needed a helping hand more than did young James.

His mother, Charlotte Hill, had been "of the gentry," but because she had committed the unpardonable sin of marrying a working man, she was disowned by her comfortably well-off people, and her pathway from then on became one of trials and hardships. In middle life, after six children had been born to them, her husband succumbed to the curse of that period—the white plague—well named in that it often wiped out whole families, and seemed to run its course unchecked wherever it chose to light. What McCarty children did not die in infancy contracted the disease, until one by one all were gone except the eldest boy, James. It was then that the distraught mother, now broken and hopeless, became reconciled to her son's departure for America. Perhaps, in that far-away land, the different climate and surroundings would give her remaining child the chance that did not seem to be coming to him at home. There, at least, he might survive. He did survive, and lived to become a real force in the building of Canada.

2

Possessed of very little education, James McCarty had a tireless thirst for learning, and it was through his persistent study during long winter evenings in his lonely backwoods cabin, where his Pennsylvania Dutch wife, Hannah Stoner, early came to share his lot, that he acquired a good foundation of English, and other subjects necessary to make him later a forceful speaker both as a politician and preacher. Perhaps it was the spirit of that gentle-bred, educated and refined mother of his back in Ireland, urging him to do honour to his ancestry, that made James McCarty a local authority on such subjects as astronomy, as well as the more orthodox matters of history and current politics.

Grandchildren, to this day, recall how fascinating the bewhiskered old man could make the starry heavens, when he took them out into the night and pointed out for them the various constellations, the outstanding stars and the planets, knowing each and all by name, and how the McCarty juniors came to appreciate Grandfather's favourite Sunday text that commenced with "When I consider Thy heavens . . ." Indeed the universe, as Grandfather interpreted it, was a marvellous and limitless wonderland.

Grandfather McCarty was justifiably proud of his connection with John A. Macdonald and early Canadian politics. It was typical of that time that a man from a backwoods log cabin, who earned his living by day-long swinging of his axe, and who had very little schooling, should be the friend and ally of this moulder of Canadian destiny. He could talk to the country electorate. He understood their language, and that he was away from home on long speaking tours, electioneering for the Conservative leader, was verified not only by his sons and daughters, but by his irate wife, Hannah, who resented being left at home with her brood of ten children, while James was out saving the country.

As a little girl, Margo used to sit at Grandmother's feet and get her to tell about her life in the little log cabin that Grandfather built for her as a bride, behind a high stockade in the Ontario woods. She told her that the big trees hung so low over their cabin that the smoke from their chimney scorched the leaves and branches. Grandmother had a pet deer which had grown so tame through its daily visits to the creek that ran past their gate that it would take a carrot from her hand. To her great grief it was shot by a hunter in its death-dodging leap over their stockade, to fall dead at her feet. How she hated that hunter.

It was in this setting that the Pioneer was born and grew to school age, and here follows his story of Ontario School days in 1870.

CHAPTER II

Ontario School Days
in 1870

Young Albert McCarty, along with his nine brothers and sisters, received all the book learning that he ever got in the old log schoolhouse which, in the winter time had as many as eighty pupils all in one room, including all grades. Albert's years of learning lasted from the age of six to ten, when his father decided that it was time he left school and went to work on the farm.

Albert agreed. If he had enough education to enable him to reckon up the value of a load of wheat, and hold his own with the town storekeeper when it came to bargaining over the price of a veal, that was adequate! He felt very proud that he was considered a man, able to take a man's place on the land, at the venerable age of ten.

The log schoolhouse had been built by local labour, paid for by the government, for Ontario was a progressive province and believed in education for its young.

The school had desks in the centre of the room, where the older pupils often sat four to a seat. Here the seniors learned their three R's, and anything more that the teacher was able to impart. There were grown men, up to thirty years of age, at school in the winter; some of them learning to read and write for the first time.

The beginners and juniors had benches all around the

walls, and their school equipment consisted of a slate and pencil. They wrote with the slate on their knees, for there was not even a table provided. When the precious slate was not in use, it was put under the bench, and woe betide the pupil who got careless with his feet and stuck his copper-rimmed heel into the slate. It was a serious matter to replace a broken article in those days. The method of cleaning one lesson off the slate to make room for another was simple, if not sanitary. A bit of good warm spittle and the edge of the hand were all that was necessary. Later, a really priggish teacher came along who insisted on bottles of water and slate cloths, and the day of complex living had begun.

From all accounts, the teacher's time was chiefly taken up in trying to maintain some semblance of order. With such a round of classes to put through the mill, and eighty restless individuals to deal with, his chances of producing brilliant results were pretty slim. His birch rod or his strap had to be freely used if he were going to make himself heard at all, and used they were.

One teacher Albert recalls with great affection. His name was McTavish. He was fair, if strict. He could sense a misdemeanour with his back turned. Albert remembers the last chastisement he got from him. He had merely stuffed a paper wad in the ear of Lucy Welsh in front of him, but the teacher had, miraculously seen this friendly gesture of attention to the pig-tailed towhead. For this offense Albert was made to kneel for an hour at the front of the room, getting a whack with the strap every time he weakened and sat down on his heels.

Then the good man reasoned with Albert. Why was it that he had had to "lick" him every day for a week? He was getting tired of it. Wasn't Albert? The teacher hoped this one would be the last.

It was the last, so far as Mr. McTavish was concerned, for his application for a raise of salary from $80 a year to $90 was deemed an ungrateful affront to the generosity and fair-mindedness of the local guardians of learning. Did a man never know when he was well off? Free board, provided successively from one cabin to another, coupled with $80 a year in spending money, should have satisfied any man—especially one following such an easy calling as pedagoguery.

Mr. James, the succeeding teacher, proved much less popular with pupils than had Mr. McTavish. While the tired Scotchman had never been guilty of pettiness, Mr. James saw fit to make mountains out of trifles. He sometimes made a crime of that which should have been applauded.

Such was the case in the matter involving pretty Alice Graham.

She had an unusual gift for drawing. Her talent won her many admiring remarks from interested swains, and when Alice started to draw on the blackboard at noon all the school looked and waited.

It was the day she drew a series of cartoons of Mr. James that things came to a head. She pictured him in collar and harness dragging a heavy cart load of St. Vincent school children up the hill of fame. He had a hard struggle in successive pictures, and finally, right at the top of the hill, his harness broke, and cart and harness rolled back down the steep incline, pupils included.

There stood Mr. James, alone on the summit, wearing nothing of the harness but the collar.

To improve on this pictured story one of the boys added a flourish of poetry:

> *Mr. James slipped his hames,*
> *Kicked over the dashboard,*
> *And ran away with the collar.*

Alice was, of course, all for rubbing the pictures off the board before the unsuspecting teacher returned, but the big boys pulled her away and kept her prisoner until he arrived.

His sense of humour, or his appreciation of real talent, was evidently entirely missing. He was very wroth. In cold, stern tones he called the school to order and demanded that the culprit confess.

Alice, a sensitive, timid girl of seventeen, grew pale; but she hesitated not at all. Rising bravely, she proclaimed in steady tones, "I am the guilty one."

Mr. James was taken aback. Alice was one of his few favourites. She was not the culprit he wanted to deal with. This time he could not go through with his intended commotion, so merely commanded curtly—

"Sit down," and he himself rubbed the work of art from the board.

There were many times when mischief really demanded a stern hand, however—that day, for example, when Farmer Harrison went by with a load of peas, headed for market. He did not know that one of the young hoodlums had climbed up on the back of his wagon as he passed the noisy school-house at the noon hour, nor that one of his sacks of peas was missing as he continued on his way.

Eighty pupils could have a lot of fun with a sack of peas, and the evidence, apparent by the time Mr. James returned, showed that the battle had been hot and effective.

The floor was a slippery mess of green peas, mashed or whole, whichever you preferred. Peas fell from the pant legs of even the tallest pupil, indicating how handfuls had made their way from collar to trouser cuff. Little girls had peas in their hair, and there were peas all over the teacher's desk.

How Mr. James dealt with this situation would take too long to relate, but the incident serves to illustrate how roughly went the way of education in those days, and how slim were the chances of a pupil emerging with any great book knowledge.

Despite these handicaps, however, young Albert in his four years at St. Vincent's brought out with him mental possessions which he always treasured very highly, and which have been of endless service to him.

It was very easy for him to memorize, and even to his last years he had a poem or a quotation to fit every occasion. Either from his own reader, or from hearing the senior students recite their lessons, he had learned poem after poem.

And that his knowledge of arithmetic was sufficient to enable him to reckon the value of a load of wheat was proven in the creditable business he in later years built up in Vancouver in his grain elevator.

Albert McCarty, like many others of his time, went further in the business and ethical world than many men who had had a much better education.

According to the Pioneer, other industries claiming the attention of these busy settlers included soap making. Piles of ashes obtained from burning slash or other surplus wood, were put through a leach until lye emerged. Combined with fats stripped from the intestines of animal carcasses, or from drippings obtained in the home, the lye made excellent soap, albeit not the kind to foster soft, velvety hands.

Albert had memories of his mother doing her week's washing for a family of ten children at the brook; rough stones serving in lieu of the not-yet-discovered washboard. So strenuous was this task that sometimes she would faint beside her work. Yet it was this same overworked, under-privileged mother who lived to within three months of being a hundred.

The women worked in the garden and in the fields. They trudged ten miles or more on foot to town to trade their basket of butter or their few dozen fresh eggs for what necessities the store would exchange for such products. Ten cents a dozen was a common price for eggs, with butter proportionately low.

Within the house there was weaving and spinning, sewing and mending, not to mention the endless days of bread making, churning, and cleaning and scrubbing. Work was from day-light to dark, whether within or without the house, and the greatest crime (next, perhaps, to lack of cleanliness) was a tendency to weaken in the treadmill. Laziness was one of the most unforgivable sins; one to call down utter contempt on the offender.

Release from toil came only on Sundays. Then man and beast alike ceased from their labours, to reverence the Sabbath rather than to rest themselves. Double work was done on Saturday. Within the home the women saw to it that all shoes were blackened and set in order for the morrow. Fresh clothes were laid out, and such a store of baking produced as would indicate provision for an expected army.

And an invasion there always was on Sunday. "The boys" were allowed to bring home their friends after church, and "the girls" were free to fetch their beaux. Tables were extended to accommodate twenty or more, and groaned under the plenitude of home grown vegetables, home cured ham, pickles, pies, tarts—everything which a well-brought-up country woman knew how to produce. Hospitality was the order of the day, and no guest was allowed to depart until he had partaken to the physical limit of everything that the pantry divulged.

Then, there was the milk house waiting for afternoon diversion. Albert recalled how "the gang" used to crowd in, or about, this cool, stone storehouse, built over the spring, and there further indulge in gorgings. The sampling of more tarts, doughnuts, cookies, pies, etc., seemed to defy every law of restraint or consequence which today holds dire threat for such over-indulgence.

Albert's recollections were punctuated by such highlights as the big race after Jeff Jenkins' funeral. The minister, rising to required heights in extolling virtues which old Jeff never possessed, and which everyone knew he never possessed, dragged out his oration too long even for these obedient and patient sons and daughters of the soil, and on this occasion a terrible reaction set in.

It was because Mos Kidd tried to pass Nick Claxtion's well behaving geldings on the way home that the race started.

Nick figured he want goin' to take a back seat to Mos even after a funeral, and before long the whole cortege, which but a few hours before had wound its way soberly and in hushed decorum all the long way from church to graveyard—in perfect order and propriety—soon was engaged in a bedlam of galloping feet, of whirling wheels, of shouting men and lashing whips.

What a spectacle—and so soon after a funeral! Black-gloved, alpaca-clad women, vested with all the solemnity befitting the occasion, now found themselves bouncing about on high wagon seats, clinging desperately to flapping bonnets and screaming babies, while all the while their men folk, reverting in an instant to the primitive, paused not till the victor had been established and the vanquished had turned off into their respective side roads to repent at leisure and digest as best they might the indignant upbraidings of their outraged spouses.

Albert remembered, too his own big sin.

Brought up a strict Methodist, dancing was to him and all the good sons who comprised this one-and-only-right religion an evil to be studiously avoided, and Albert had scrupulously obeyed to the letter his relentless schooling in this connection.

It was not until he—an intense lover of music—was led by the evil one to let his steps come nearer and nearer to the source of those sweet, rhymthic strains of fiddle and flute that finally he came within view of the most fascinating sight he had ever beheld.

The outdoor pavilion, set up in the beautiful forest, leafy bowered, lantern-lit, presented a picture of swaying forms, bright-hued summer frocks, smoothly gliding partners with graceful girls in their arms, all floating, whirling, weaving in and out of an intricate pattern in perfect attunement with the music. Albert was enthralled.

Before that night was over he had made a deadly resolve—he was going to learn to dance!

Now a young man, in measure exercising some will of his own, he was deaf to entreaty, command or threat of home or church, and for a whole summer he was part of that magical company, following the musicians through reel or jig, through waltz or Roger de Coverley, permitting no twinge of conscience or fear of consequence to mar the unalloyed delight of this new-found indulgence in the poetry of motion.

It was not until one of those all-powerful camp meetings came along when mighty men of the Lord, equipped with oratory and the power of persuasion, worked in teams and in relays to rouse whole neighbourhoods to a sense of their own wickedness and their need of regeneration that Albert came face to face with a realization of the error of his course, and stepped down forever from the paths of pleasure which he was so joyously entering.

Life held more serious things for the young Canadian, as the long years ahead were to prove.

CHAPTER III

Lost in the Backwoods

A ny Canadian still living who had personal knowledge of the early Ontario backwoods, or who learned from the lips of a reminiscing forefather something of the danger that lurked for the unwary in the confusing labyrinth of forest and swamp which constituted the topography of that province in the last century, can appreciate the terror which the word "lost" could strike in the hearts of the early pioneers. The story of Mary Kendall, vividly recalled by the Pioneer, well illustrates the upheaval of the neighbourhood which took place when any member of the community became lost in the maze of undergrowth for which the Canadian backwoods was noted.

Most of these tales, Margo had heard years ago. It was when the wind howled outside and shook their gaunt frame farmhouse to its foundations in one of those wild Manitoba blizzards, that the Pioneer was at his best. As if to minimize the grim terror of the storm outside, he would pile more wood on the roaring fire, and then begin to remember.

It was on one of those mellow late-summer evenings that the Kendall cows came home without Mary an hour after she had set out to look for them, immediately shattering the peace of that tranquil Ontario farmstead.

"Fred and I will go find her," father Kendall had agreed, "and you start the milking" (to his worried wife). "We'll be back directly to finish up the heifers. You can't handle them."

Kendall and his son came back as promised at sundown, but Mary was not with them.

"Get the lantern," the big bewhiskered farmer ordered. "Fred you go borrow another from John."

John, next door neighbour half a mile away, not only found Fred a lantern but volunteered to go with him. Word spread that little Mary Kendall, thirteen-year-old pride of the neighbourhood, had not come back from fetching the cows, and before midnight a dozen men and boys were out looking for her.

The night was dark, not even stars providing guidance and the search was laborious.

Over fallen logs, through quagmires, into dense thickets went the lantern bearers, hallooing and calling "Mary" as they hunted.

The searchers repeatedly came back to the Kendall farm to see if any word had come of the lost child, then fanned out into the blackness in an organized drive to find the young girl before morning.

It was indeed a lonesome night for a child of thirteen to be out, for all knew there were timber wolves, and bears in the woods.

Morning came and Mary had not been found. The alarm spread further afield; women and children took up the search as long as the daylight lasted.

"We'll be finding her today," all agreed, little knowing that for fourteen long days and nights the heart-breaking search was to continue until the entire neighbourhood, and adjoining districts, were included in the stupendous task of learning what had befallen blue-eyed, golden-haired Mary Kendall, a maid small for her years and as timid as she was gentle.

There were prayer meetings. Groups met in private houses, in the district schoolhouse, and in the churches, to pray for the lost girl's safe return.

Horrible visions of Mary in the clutches of a bear, or, being mauled by a vicious timber wolf, haunted the distraught mother to the limit of human endurance, and fell like a heavy pall in varying degrees on the heart of every man, woman and child in the district.

"She was such a nice girl," her schoolmates agreed as they plodded patiently through the thickets.

Tom Loree, the tall youth of sixteen who was known to have been especially fond of Mary, had nothing at all to say as he walked and looked, looked and shouted, usually by himself, tirelessly coming back to the Kendall home for possible good news. That he did not go home at all except to snatch some more sandwiches was averred by those who watched the fast-thinning boy. They did not believe he ever stopped to sleep, even in the woods.

"Don't take it so hard, lad," Mary's father had advised, coming upon him one afternoon fighting his way through swamp underbrush.

"We can't all kill ourselves just to find the lass. Although God knows I would die to locate her."

"And so would I," snapped the tight-lipped youth as he darted off to hide the blinding tears.

It was one of the doubting Thomases who voiced what many felt.

"All this prayin'," he pondered. "Do you s'pose the Lord really cares what's become of Mary? Do you s'pose He gives a hoot—whether she's et up or lyin' sick and hurt under some log?"

"Aw shut up," had been his rebuke from another unbeliever. "Give the Lord a chance. He may be lookin' after her as good as her mother."

Mrs. Kendall meanwhile was prostrate. As the days dragged by, sleepless night following tormented day, she drooped and failed, until she finally had to go to bed, with neighbours to wait on her.

Men stopped their work in the fields, dropping everything to devote their whole time to finding Mary Kendall. Schools shrank to half their size as the older boys and girls became volunteers in the search.

Gratitude for the interest taken in his daughter grew in Kendall's heart, and gripped him at the throat.

So full of this display of kindness was he that he had almost forgotten to hate old Jim McDonald when he passed his silent house at the end of ten days of weary looking.

No fear of Jim being with the searchers! Jim and he hadn't spoken for eight years, not since that awful fight they had had over the line fence.

There was a glint from another lantern tonight as Kendall stumbled through the underbrush. The bushes parted and a weary searcher staggered toward him.

The two men held the lanterns to each other's face.

Kendall saw before him—Jim McDonald!

Silently the two men stared into each other's eyes.

It was Kendall who first found his voice.

"You too, Jim?" he said huskily. He held out his hand. The other grasped it and they looked long at each other. Neither could say more. Each knew that their long quarrel was at an end.

"I'm taking the lower swamp. You take the alder grove," Jim growled finally, his voice gruff with emotion.

The men parted and Kendall went on. A great load seemed lifted from him.

"Miracles do happen," he mumbled, and continued his search with new strength and new hope.

Meanwhile—what had been happening to Mary?

All had gone fairly well until she had taken that new path. There were fresh cow tracks ahead of her, and she was sure they indicated her five—two with big hoofs—Brindle and Blossom—and three with small hoofs—the heifers. But here at the swamp's edge they had left the path and waded into the shallow water. She thought she could pick up the trail just on the other side, so took off her shoes and stockings to paddle the warm, stagnant pools.

On the other side no tracks were to be found. She searched, and soon could not even find the way back whence she had come. Little Gyp, the part Collie, had barked excitedly, apparently bent on leading her in quite the wrong direction.

It was not until weeks later when Mary revisited the spot to go over the whole story with her father, that she realized that Gyp had known what he was about, and the whole trouble had been in failing to trust his judgment.

"You're smart, Gyp," his little mistress told him now, "but you're wrong this time. This is the way back."

And with youthful determination she laid her course in quite the opposite direction to that advised by the yapping Gyp.

It did not take long from this point for Mary Kendall to realize she was hopelessly lost.

Terror filled her. Only from such an admission can such hopeless alarm come.

By this time even Gyp seemed confused, and when the lost girl sat down on a log and wept copiously all he could do was excitedly lick her face and plead with her not to take it so hard.

"We'll get out of this jam, some way," he seemed to be admonishing. "And anyway, you've got me. I'll stay with you."

And it was Gyp's presence with her all through the terrible fourteen days that followed that kept Mary's courage alive and made this terror of the woods bearable.

He slept at her feet at night. Or, when it was cold and Mary gathered him in her arms for warmth, he cuddled close against her body, his tail beating a tattoo on the ground and his tongue ready to proffer a comforting kiss. If only Mary wouldn't cry he could stand anything else.

Wild berries and nuts were Mary's only food during those fourteen days. Gyp fared better, for he caught squirrels; and his eagerness to have Mary share them with him was pathetic. He would come bounding up, his dog face all smiles, and drop a dead squirrel at Mary's feet. Then with joyous barks he would circle around her, plainly saying—

"There's your dinner, little pal."

Starved as Mary was, she could not bring herself to touch the raw meat, and she had no means of lighting a fire.

Back and forth, up and down through the swamp she wandered. Elm, ash, basswood, maples and beech trees grew in a maze of confusion along the water's edge, providing shelter from the hot sun in the daytime, and some manner of covering for her and Gyp at night.

Wolves howled dismally in the dark, and there were strange crackling sounds in the bushes occasionally that made Mary grip Gyp to her in terror. That must be a bear!

Never, however, were the two strays molested by wild animals. It was after some days of wandering that Mary realized she must follow the stream down if she wished to ever get back to her father's farm.

But this swampy creek ran so slowly it was next to impossible to tell which way it travelled; and indeed part of the surface moved in one direction and the further side in another.

It was very difficult to tell which was up-stream or down.

Hunger almost proved Mary's downfall on one occasion, when she climbed a hill to pick some promising beech nuts. One tree lured her on to another, until she realized that she was again losing sight of her creek.

Greater care was exercised after that to make sure the "stream", such as it was, never passed from her range of vision.

Always she prayed.

"Dear God, I'm here all alone with you. You must take me home."

She was very cold some nights, despite the best Gyp could do to get her warm. She dreamed in her slumber of the warm bed awaiting her at home, and dry sobs would awaken her. Would this NEVER end!

It was on the fourteenth day that Mrs. Green was shaking the table cloth at the back door of the Kendall home. She had prepared supper for Mr. Kendall and Fred, and taken Mrs. Kendall an untouched tray.

But, now out shaking the table cloth, Mrs. Green was suddenly aroused from the deadly numbness that gripped her—that same devastating suspense which pervaded the whole home—by a slight movement in the lane leading to the barn.

Her sight was not very good—but—this did look like a girl. It looked like a girl with tattered clothing, barefoot, with a little dog leading her on.

Mrs. Green, old and staid as she was, gave a war whoop.

"Mattie, Mattie," she shouted to the half-conscious Mrs. Kendall. "Mattie, wake up—it's Mary—IT'S MARY!"

Then the woman who had not been able to rise from her couch for a week sat up. She flung herself out of bed and grasped her neighbour by both shoulders.

"You're tellin' me the truth, are you?" she demanded harshly.

"Honest to God, Mattie Kendall. Look for yourself."

The excited woman pushed the incredulous mother to the door.

There it was—a little wisp of a figure, a brush of matted hair visible even from this distance, a little dog that looked like Gyp preceding her.

It was Mary!

Without a word Mrs. Kendall dashed from the house in her night clothes. Her two legs which had not been able to bear her weight for days now sped down the lane.

By this time Father Kendall, at the barn, had seen, too. He came running. So did Fred. So did the hired man.

The joy of Gyp broke all bounds. He ran to meet them, barking uproariously. He dashed back to Mary. He circled her with mad yelps. He went quite crazy with unalloyed rapture. Mary was found!

And Mary? Trembling she watched them near her. She could go no further. She stood motionless. Then her knees gave way, and she sank to the ground.

It was a light little body they carried back to the house, with life apparently extinct. Words of endearment, loving caresses, tears of joy now mingled with fear were lavished on the prostrate form as Mary lay stretched on the couch.

Nourishment was poured into scarcely yielding lips, and for days Mary hovered between life and death.

But she was home! The awful uncertainty as to her fate was gone, and even this was better than the torture the family had endured the past fortnight.

And finally Mary's eyes opened one day to recognize her mother.

"I knew He would bring me back to you," breathed the little girl as her arms stole about her mother's neck. The depth and joy of that moment was shared by the father and brother, who blubbered unashamedly.

When the whole long story of her wanderings could be told it was little Gyp who was the hero. Tired to exhaustion, he asked only the privilege of lying quietly at Mary's feet, to sleep, and sleep.

"You'll never lack a home from me, you little piebald mongrel," big Kendall had averred as he held the paws of the happy dog in his great hands.

And who was the most honoured visitor to the Kendall home?

Kendall had caught sight of him at the gate. He had come up hesitatingly, his face a study.

Kendall had merely stepped to the door and held it open for the man who had not crossed his threshold in eight years.

"She'll be glad to see you; and you used to be fond of her," Kendall had said in a low, throaty voice; but when he saw the tears in the eyes of his former avowed enemy his eyes also filled.

There were more prayer meetings in the neighbourhood, this time of thanksgiving. And for the first time in his young life Tom Loree was there, sitting very close to Mary, his long slim face serious as ever but with a deep light of joy in his eyes.

CHAPTER IV

The Big Fight at the Camp Meeting

T he Pioneer was only fourteen years old when the big
fight at the Camp Meeting occurred. The chief charm
of this story, in the estimation of his daughter, was in
hearing him tell it. Sitting among his cushions, the big invalid
recalled the camp meeting battle with a pride that brought a
glow to his cheek and fire to his still-bright eyes.

"My father was in it," he said, excitedly, "and wasn't I
proud of him!"

His father, James McCarty, was counted on by all the travelling evangelists to do what they themselves ofttimes could
not accomplish—move sinners to repentance in gratifying
droves.

Methodist camp meetings were the event of the year to
hundreds in the old backwoods days. Regular ministers
gathered up lay-ministers as they moved from one district
to another, until they numbered as many as ten men of God.
These, together and in turn, put on day-long campaigns
against the devil and all his works; hundreds flocking to the
big tents to listen, to see, to ridicule, or to yield to the fire of
the orators and throw themselves in capitulation at the
campaigners' feet.

These were noisy sessions. Members of more staid
denominations roundly condemned the carryings-on of the

camp meetings, and the hard part of it was that ofttimes those who came to scoff remained to pray. It got even the most scornful of the orthodox, and the most sinful of sinners.

There were unique figures among the evangelists. The Pioneer remembered one famous preacher, Lorenzo Dowe. Anyone surviving from that day will recall the name and remember what a mighty man of God he was, albeit quite a freak in appearance and actions.

He was tall, and gaunt. He wore his ministerial coat buttoned about his thin form in emphasizing tightness. He had long hair that followed him like an attached halo as he darted about the platform, going through antics that certainly arrested attention if not always occasioning admiration.

The chief eccentricity about Lorenzo (and he had many) was his habit of wearing two hats. Both tall silk stove-pipers they were; the best one underneath with the second one worn on top to protect the first from the weather.

Lorenzo's prominent nose and large ears gave him a marked resemblance to his majesty, the devil, so many thought.

Lorenzo Dowe would probably have been a past-master at gaining attention in the movie business, for he had drastic ways of attracting notice. One story reveals his methods.

On his round of visitation he had come upon wicked Spike Harris, cruelly beating his oxen. The poor animals were stalled on Mud Hill, knee deep in mire, their impossible load holding them from further progress while their infamous master vented his wrath upon them with a heavy club.

Spike was known as a bad man. His little wife had suffered at his hands, for he was a drunkard as well as a meanie. Her one desire had been to get him to the camp meetings, that he might be saved, as had so many of his hard fisted neighbours. If only she could get Lorenzo Dowe on his trail, all would be well, she knew.

And now here was Lorenzo Dowe, with the prospective subject before him.

Lorenzo's methods were always original, and in this case he ran true to type.

He came up behind Spike and tapped him on the shoulder.

"You're doing fine, my friend," gloated the long thin stranger. Spike turned around and saw what looked very much like Mephistopheles leering at him over his shoulder, his black eyes regarding him gloatingly.

"Yes, you're doing fine, my friend. Just keep it up, and you're mine. And here's a dollar to show you that I've bought you. And," added this strange apparition, "of course your oxen can't pull that load over the hill, and if you really want to get them out you will take them first down the hill, then around by that other road. Goodbye, my friend; and remember," with a final jubilant gloat, "I've bought you. From henceforth you're mine."

It was a dazed and disturbed Spike that finally arrived home, having mechanically followed the advice of the devil about getting his oxen out of the mud.

"What's the matter, Spike?" enquired his wife, her feminine intuition quick to recognize that something out of the ordinary had happened to Spike.

He sat down on the chopping block at the door and said in a bewildered voice—

"I've sold myself to the devil—here is his dollar. He says I'm his."

From this point it was not a difficult task for the wife to persuade Spike that now indeed it was time he went to the camp meeting and got converted.

When he meekly followed his wife down the "aisle," where about three hundred noisy worshippers were already filling the plank and log seats, his astonishment was unbounded.

"That's the man," he whispered excitedly—"that's the devil. That's the one I sold myself to."

The versatile Lorenzo was equal to the occasion. Catching sight of Spike he hurried toward him.

"Yes, my friend, I've bought you, but not for the devil. I've bought you for the Lord—for life! Follow me. He has great work for you to do. You'll be a great worker in His vineyard."

And so it proved. Spike then and there got religion, and his drinking, his tantrums, his violence for which he had long been condemned, disappeared and he was henceforth a changed man.

That was the way things were going. So many of these bad men of the woods, were getting converted at the camp meetings, with resultant loss of trade at the village saloons, that the "trade" in town decided they must do something about it.

The whiskey men got together and agreed that this thing of putting their best customers on the water wagon had gone about far enough. They drew up a plan.

Out at the camp in the woods a whisper went around that Gregan's tavern was sending out a bunch of hooligans to break up the meetings. The eight preachers then in charge of this very busy camp held a prayer meeting and decided to enlist the service of the Lord in combating the threat.

The hooligans indeed came, and they were indeed tanked up and ready to cause all the grief to the reverend brethren which a dozen drunks could accomplish. The preachers tried to ignore the marauders and go on with their meetings. They endured interruptions, mockery of those who got up to testify, exaggerated mimicry of the songs, and other disturbances designed to tax to the limit the patience of even holy men pledged at all times and under all circumstances to exercise Christian forbearance.

"Glory to God! Another sinner down!" was one of the favourite shouts of the ruffians as they mocked an ardent thanksgiver.

There were no police to whom to appeal, and it was pretty hard when the bullies even horned in on the eating tables under the trees outside, snatching victuals, and making themselves thoroughly obnoxious. The ministers commanded patience.

"If thine enemy smite thee on one cheek, turn him also the other," quoted the long-suffering pastors as they sought to continue their work.

Things came to a head the afternoon when burly Steve Bowden went one too far. Right in the middle of prayer he broke into the meeting and sat down on the rough-hewn plank bench beside Curly Mason's wife, attempting to kiss her. It was Pastor Cragg who was on his knees, exhorting divine riddance of this plague that had come upon them when this impossible situation developed. Pastor Cragg had been a pugilist in his day, and one eye opened as Mrs. Mason fought off the advances of the drunken lout. Then Pastor Cragg's coat was coming off and he was on his feet.

"Who'll follow me?" he shouted. Instantly everyone was in action, all over the big tent. The free-for-all that followed is what set the Old Pioneer's eyes dancing as he described the melée, seventy-two years after it happened.

Fired with righteous wrath, charged with supernatural strength from the very necessity of the situation, these men of God, eight strong, waded into the rowdies with all the ardour of holy fury. Down they went—the gang from town— over benches, into aisles, against yielding tent walls. Women and children fell to the sidelines, and there cheered their menfolk, most of whom were in the battle before it was finished.

Finally victorious, the righteous warriors chased the unwanted gang into the yard and on to their horses. They pursued them down the road, yelling and shouting their triumph as, bloody and bowed, the ruffians fled.

It was when one of the vanquished, hastening to escape from this unexpected display of vengeance, got his horse into a mire-hole and there floundered that—

"Glory to God!" shouted exulting Pastor Cragg, "Another sinner down!"

"And my father was one of the best of the bunch!" gloated the Pioneer as the picture all came back to him.

When order was finally restored in the blood-stained tent, the question was, who should preach.

"I can't preach," and "I can't preach," came from the panting pastors. It was long, thin Lorenzo Dowe who answered this challenge.

"I CAN!" he shouted, and he mounted the platform and thundered forth his text—

"And the gates of hell shall not prevail against them!"

Record has it that more souls were saved after this display of ministerial fistic prowess than were harvested in a single season before.

"They talked about it for years in our neighbourhood," says the Pioneer. "The Lord was wholly victorious!"

Yes, religion was vital in those days.

CHAPTER V

When a Wedding Day
was an Adventure

I t was because the Pioneer's sixty-fourth wedding anniversary came around whilst he sat in his convalescent chair, in
his daughter's Lulu Island home, that he got to reminiscing
about his wedding day.

Quite different was this rain-drenched day of January third,
1947, away out here on the Western coast, from that far-distant
January third, 1883, when snow drifts and blizzards in old
Ontario had almost prevented the marriage as planned.

The Pioneer's wife, still living in the family home in
Vancouver under the care of her youngest son, had been
expected to join her husband on Lulu Island, on this ripe
anniversary (one which relatively few couples attain), but the
heavy rain had made her choose her own fireside in preference to another wedding anniversary involving a slippery
drive. She had had so many celebrations—sixty-three of
them—the diamond anniversary of four years ago having been
a thing of such pomp and splendour as to serve as a grand
finale to the long, long series.

The Pioneer had not forgotten any detail of that memorable
day, and of his wife he now reminisced:

"She was the prettiest girl in the village. I am afraid she was
often disappointed in me, and what I could give her. She was
really cut out for the town, not the farm."

She sang in the choir, in the active town of Meaford. She took part in young people's activities. According to the Pioneer, she was very popular. Small of waist, rosy of cheek, black of hair and snappy of eye, she was indeed the belle of the set in which she moved, and Albert scarcely knew why she accepted him. On the other hand, Margo had learned from aunts of that period that Father was no slouch at love-making. His handsome, six-foot-two stature, his jovial good-nature, his fine tenor voice, all combined to turn the head of many a village miss, and Harriett was the envy of many a girl when her engagement was announced.

Leaving his farm on this stormy January third, 1883, with stout-hearted grey Tom between the shafts of the home-made cutter, Albert and his mother set out on their long, hazardous ride to Walter's Falls, and matrimony. The wind was blowing a gale, and little could be seen beyond a cutter's length. The snow whirled in their faces in choking gusts, and Tom had all he could do to stay on the road. Great drifts made travelling a snail's pace, but Tom took them all till he came to Smith's Corner. Here the wind, sweeping around the apple orchard, had piled a wall of whiteness across the dim trail. Tom stopped in his tracks, snorting. He turned his grey head, frost hanging from every hair, to Albert, as if pleading—

"You're not asking me to go through this one, are you Boss?"

The Boss gave him an order.

"Go on, Tom; we've got to get there."

Tom stood up on his hind legs and obediently threw himself into the drift. There he stuck. He wallowed about, nearly upsetting the light cutter and its occupants, but shortly giving up and remaining in his tracks, helpless and looking back to see what Albert was going to do about it.

Albert got out and tried to tramp the snow about the imprisoned horse, vainly trying to liberate him. The snow was over the animal's flanks, however, and he was fast.

Neighbours were good in those days and, peering through

the storm, a nearby stranger took in the situation. He got out his team of oxen and came plodding to help.

"Man, you're crazy—out on a day like this!" was his terse comment.

"I've got to be out. This is my wedding day," Albert explained.

"Oh, that's different!" and forthwith the Good Samaritan set to work with a will to dig Tom out.

With the old grey's feet again near the ground, the farmer put his oxen ahead of the cutter and broke a path with them for Tom to get through the remaining bad drifts.

"It's just twenty minutes ago since I broke a road through here," the puffing volunteer shouted through the storm, "And look at it now."

No compensation was expected or collected by the friend in need. Settlers were like that in that era. Anyone in trouble was signal for impromptu assistance.

Half the invited guests could not get to the wedding because of the storm and the bad roads, but the marriage, which was the first to be performed in this new little Methodist church at Walter's Falls, took place on schedule at high noon, and a goodly number of friends and relatives witnessed the event.

The bride wore an apple green satin dress (years after to be tried on and admired by interested daughters) tight fitting at the slim waist line (made by the bride herself) and buttoned to the chin in semi-tailored effect. The wedding dinner which followed at the home of the bride's mother was such as only cooks of the old school could produce. It was served in the family home, now over a hundred years old and still in good repair.

There were more snowy adventures for the groom on his homeward way, this time with his young bride tucked into the cutter between himself and his mother. The mother was being taken back to Meaford while the bride and groom were to proceed to the farm.

A stubborn drift sent one runner of the light sleigh high into the air, and the bride flying out on to the snow. In the upset, she took the robe with her, and there sat comfortably upon the robe on the snow until assisted back into the cutter.

Another recollection, perhaps not before known to his wife, was the little matter of getting the wedding ring paid for. It took five loads of wood, cut and sawed by the groom himself, to settle that account.

There followed for the young couple six years of back-breaking, and well nigh heart-breaking, toil on the hundred acre Ontario farm.

The old original pioneer, James McCarty, the Irish immigrant, had moved with his wife and the remnants of their family to retire in the town of Meaford, and Albert took over the old farm, with its stock and implements. For six hard, grinding years he and his young wife struggled to wrest enough from the land and the five cows to pay the $300 yearly rental fee, keep the house in town in firewood and foodstuffs, and take care of the young family that started arriving very shortly.

Hours for the Pioneer were from 4 a.m. to 10 or 11 p.m., with breakfast at 6 o'clock and supper twelve hours later. Albert had never been considered a strong youth. Six-foot-two in his stocking feet he was pronounced by his tailor the thinnest man he ever made clothes for when he had his wedding suit made.

"Tired, tired—the whole blessed time I was tired—get up tired, go to bed tired," remembered the Pioneer; and for his wife there was little less toil and drudgery. It was small wonder the farmers thought labour men lazy when they started talking about a ten hour day, or more scandalous—an eight hour day. For the men on the land it was eighteen hours or more, and even at that the agriculturists could scarcely make a living.

The wife made butter from the five cows and delivered it to the home folk at Meaford to pay for the furniture that had been left them in the big old eight room farm house. She got ten cents a pound for her high class product, which was adjudged as fine as any country bred lass could have made. She, having grown up in the village, had to learn all these arts when she went to the farm. She helped with the milking, and mothered two nephews that a deceased sister-in-law had bequeathed her, making life just a daily round of toil, with none of the romance that the story books had led her to believe awaited after marriage.

One had to like work, and be able to extract pleasure from the babies and the other simple homely things of life if one was to get any happiness at all.

Albert, like his father, had a deep inborn desire to preach. Like his father, he would have been a minister of the gospel had there been any way to make the long climb to that exalted post. As it was, he had to content himself, like his father, with being a "local preacher."

James H., despite his hard weeks in the woods with his axe, or on the land after he had got it cleared, found strength to walk as much as eleven or twelve miles on a Sunday to get to his different church appointments. The horses had worked all week; they must rest on Sunday. And so it was with Albert. The horses, Tom and Johnny, were turned out in the orchard to obey the Sabbath command about resting on the seventh day, while Albert trudged on foot to his church or Sunday School.

Rising at the usual hour of 4 a.m., he would get all the chores done in time to leave him free for the bulk of the day. No, there was no way for "mother" to go, too, so she stayed home with the babies. Perhaps she wondered sometimes why she had not married that town man, for certainly the farm offered little compensation for a woman in Ontario.

If Ontario farmers acquired the reputation of being small, and mean, this fact would also not be surprising, for they gained their living the hard, hard way, with so little at the end of the year to show for their twelve months of drudgery that miserly qualities just naturally had fertile ground in which to grow.

CHAPTER VI

Bella,
the Liberated Slave

There are, still living, Canadians who can add to our early history thrilling tales of escaped slaves. These poor people were frequently discovered, cowering in terror in woods and caves of rural Ontario just north of the border, as yet unable to believe in the safety to which they had attained. One such was discovered by some schoolboys, hiding in a weed-filled culvert just outside of Dundas. He was starving, but begged the boys not to tell anybody about him, so for some days they took turns in smuggling food to him. Finally the watchful mothers became suspicious; the boys were followed, and the frightened man was rescued, reassured and properly cared for by the villagers.

Bella, however, had been liberated before she, by some means unknown to the Pioneer, made her way to Walter's Falls. Here she settled and became a popular village character. Bella's was a face that everyone in the village loved. She had an inner radiance that made her countenance shine, and she beamed goodwill on all who came in her path. She was old (no one knew how old) with hands crippled and knotted from years of overwork.

It was Bella's back, however, that told the story of her slavery. It was striped with scars, put there by the whip of her master in her final Gethsemane before her liberation. Once a minister had been reading to her the story of Paul; how in his report to a brother martyr of the early days, he had said "I bear in my body the marks of the Lord Jesus Christ."

As she drank in the words, her face lit up with that transforming light, and she said:

"That's me, Pa'son. I'se just like Mr. Paul, fo' I has de ma'ks in my body of de Lord Jesus Christ."

This idea thrilled her, and made her scars to her something to cherish and value.

That part of Bella's story is dire. It reveals the grim fact that all the cruelty and torture credited to the enemy in the recent war was not the exclusive possession of the Japanese or the Germans. To tell it briefly, Bella had been the leader of the band of slaves which toiled on the cotton farm of "Massa Grimwood." On one occasion his will and that of Bella had definitely clashed.

Bella had consistently refused to work on Sunday. She had got religion in the Free Methodist church down the lane, and she had got it bad. It made her a better worker generally, more willing to please and more cheerful. But when it came to Sunday work, she put her foot down hard.

"I cook for you. I wash yo' dishes. I make yo' bed, but I no go into de field."

When he found that she was obdurate, he had taken her into the basement, according to Bella's own story (and no one doubted it—the proof was there) and had whipped her unmercifully. As each lash cut into her dark back she breathed,

"God bless you, Massa. God forgive you, Massa."

He failed. Bella, her face uplifted in glorified persecution, withstood all until she dropped in a swoon. Then, fearing that he had killed her, he sank into a chair and trembled.

"God bless you, Massa. God forgive you, Massa," kept ringing in his ears.

The sequel to this incident (at that time such an affair was nothing but a daily incident in the South), was that

Grimwood's remorse proved genuine. He called all his slaves together and told them that he was going to set them free. How Bella got away up into Canada and into this little village which had not even a railroad, is not known to the Pioneer. She was there when he first visited the hamlet, living in her little shack under the shadow of a huge, projecting rock, supported by the generosity of town residents, augmented by produce from her small garden.

That rock made Bella quite a lot of trouble. It was only a step off the path that led to school, and boys seldom passed it without running out on the ledge and looking down at Bella's house. Some of the more mischievous had found it fun to jump down on Bella's roof as an extra diversion, particularly when they found that such procedure annoyed her and brought repercussions.

Bella's line of talk was always a source of interest to the youngsters, and they liked to hear her remonstrances.

"What fo' you boys lak to wake this ole woman up when she's jes havin' the bes' sleep that she neve' did git all dem bad years? You jes run 'long and let ole black mammy sleep."

When such protests brought only renewed visits Bella broke into prayer. She came out in her white nightdress and knelt in her front door yard. With arms upraised she prayed volubly to the Lord to "chase de debil out o' de hea'ts of des chillens dat dey may leave old mammy 'lone."

This exhibition so delighted the boys that more than ever they came, and great was their enjoyment of Bella's conversations with the Almighty.

"Once I pray," recounted Bella later telling the Pioneer all about it. "Twice I pray, and still dey come. I try de Lo'd jes once mo'. And agin dey come. Den, I puts de good Lo'd on de shelf and goes aftah dose boys wit my tomahawk!"

Villagers say that the spectacle of Bella, really aroused to righteous wrath, hotly pursuing half a dozen mischievous schoolboys, with a murderous looking weapon, was really an awesome sight. At any rate, the boys let her alone after that, and whether the village schoolmaster took a hand in the matter at that point Bella never knew. But her deduction from the incident was—

"Yes, sometimes you has to help de Lo'd jes a li'l bit."

There were times when the village boys were her best friends.

Such an occasion was one October when winter had settled in early, and Bella had no wood. She prayed about it, as she did about all her problems. She mentioned it to the Lord in her prayers in church, but nothing happened.

Then came Halloween, and in the morning, Lo—there was a lovely pile of neatly split wood in her back yard!

It did look a good deal like Mr. Banton's wood, from next door. But then one mustn't question the source of the Almighty's benefactions. There was her wood in direct answer to her prayer, and it was her part only to give thanks and rejoice.

Early in the morning she heard a noise in the back yard, and there was that Mr. Banton (one of the most prosperous men in the village, and the tightest) tossing the wood over the fence into his yard.

"What you do, what you do, Massa Banton?" Bella remonstrated.

Mr. Banton wasn't in a very good humour.

"Children nowadays haven't got any bringing up," he growled. "In my time they would be soundly whipped for a thing like this."

"What you mean, Massa Banton? What fo' you take my wood?"

"YOUR wood," said the merchant scornfully. "You know very well this is my wood that those wretched boys threw over into your yard last night. They think it's funny."

Bella planted herself squarely in front of the irate man, hands on hips.

"Massa, as sho' as Gawd's alive he done send me dat wood. If I let you take it, he'll nebah do nuttin mo' fo' me.

Yes, I know it came from yo' ya'd. But the good Lo'd put it in de boys' hea'ts to do it. It come right from de Lawd."

Mr. Banton looked at her shining face and soulful black eyes and capitulated.

"You win, Bella," he said grimly, and went his way.

It was at the time of the Chicago fire in the summer of 1871 that Bella set a worthy example to all the terrified villagers of Walter's Falls.

Margo's mother, then eleven-year-old Harriett Caswell, native of this little hamlet, had been with Bella the day the sky turned to blood.

Harriett had told her daughter about it years ago.

She and Bella were thinning turnips together in Mr. Wagstaff's field, working among the stumps for 35 cents each per day. The sky had been unduly red in the morning, and had occasioned much comment and speculation as the villagers greeted each other on their way to work. As the day progressed, the glow became deeper and deeper, until by mid-afternoon the whole arch above them from horizon to horizon was a blood crimson. By this time most of the townspeople had stopped their work. They assembled in groups on the street, to gaze with mystified and fear-filled faces at the awesome spectacle.

Yes, there was something in the Bible about the sky turning to blood when the last day should come. What else could this be but the final hour?

Some took to their knees, remembering their great wickednesses, and prayed mightily for forgiveness. Others crowded into the church where the pastor, himself mystified and not a little alarmed, made capital of the prevailing terror and got scores to the altar who had never been there before. Little children, sensing their elders' alarm, huddled against their mothers and cried pitifully.

Harriett recalled Bella's calm as the day wore on.

She had paused in her work for a few moments occasionally, to gaze at the crimson heavens. She manifested no alarm.

Instead, a great peace and joy seemed to take possession of her. Finally, she said:

"It looks like He was a'comin'—fo' shuah dis time He's a'comin'—and you, honey chile—you and me is goin' to be took togedder. Glory me!" Bella's face fairly shone.

"But—" she went on, returning to her work. "He ain't goin' to catch me slackin' on de job. Black Bella al'ays done he' dooty. Come on, honey chile, you and I must git dis job done afore He gits heah!"

And she set to work with a greater will to finish her day's stint.

When the villagers heard that Bella, the most superstitious and emotional individual in the district, was calmly thinning turnips as the possible end drew near, they became calmer, and in many cases decided to adopt Bella's wait-and-see attitude.

Next day they learned that Chicago was on fire, and the terrifying reflection in the sky was explained. One and all thereupon set out to convince the other that really, he or she had not been so very frightened after all.

Bella was full of good works, going about the village when anyone was in trouble and doing whatever she could to lend a hand.

When she learned that the Pioneer had gone away out there to Manitoba, and that his "honey" and her three children were soon too follow, she was most solicitous.

"I heah dey has hard fellowships out in dat country," she sympathized, and she proffered her warmest shawl in which to wrap the six-weeks' old baby.

It was in church that Bella really enjoyed herself. Her religion was one of warm emotion, and it broke all bounds; so much so that ministers learned never to ask her to pray. The dignity of this village sanctuary could scarcely stand Bella's high ecstasies and her voluble conversations with the Almighty.

A new minister came to the village, however, and he was not forewarned.

At the Wednesday evening prayer meeting he called on some brother or sister to pray. Immediately Bella was in the aisle, on her knees.

With arms raised she let loose, pouring forth her soul to heaven.

"Come down through the roof, Lo'd," she entreated. "Come right in heah whe' we is and fill us plumb full o' you'self."

Her ardour increased as her prayer progressed. She went the full length of the aisle to the altar on her knees, waving her arms aloft and praising the Lord.

"Yes, I know, Gawd," she told him. "You's sent us heaps and heaps o' blessin's. But the's all gone. They's all et up an' all wore out. We need some mo'."

"An' this new man o' Gawd you done send us," she entreated. "He's the sheph'd o' de flock and we's all goin' to eat gwass in de same pastu' togedder. Glory to Gawd, and glory to Gawd!"

Many an eye opened forbiddenly to take a look to learn how the dapper new preacher was taking this. They found he also had an eye open, not missing anything of Bella's performance. Far from being shocked, the young man evidently was enjoying the demonstration. He shook hands heartily with Bella after the meeting and thanked her for her wonderful prayer. He found out where she lived and promised to call.

"You're full of the spirit," he told the old woman. She was listening very intently. "But couldn't you make your prayers just a little more refined?"

"What you mean, Pa'son?"

"Well, your grammar, for example. Couldn't you use a little better grammar."

Bella was interested.

"O, I see, Pa'son," she blinked thoughtfully. Then her face broke into one of her irresistible smiles.

"Youse right, Pa'son. I knowse my pra's doesn't go up grammah, but de comes down grammah!"

The young man soon gave up trying to reform Bella's diction, and learned, like his predecessors, to restrict her to occasional outbursts.

At such times she was apt to come out with such glorified exultation as this:

"Ise so full o' joy I could talk a whole hour dis blessed minute!"

Or—

"I won't be black no mo', no mo', when I gits on dose silber slippers and a-walkin' dose golden streets."

Probably the largest funeral ever held in Walter's Falls was recorded when Bella died.

Very old, she had been able to get about and look after herself until her call came one night while she slept. When they found her in her bed, life departed, there was a radiant smile on her face.

"She may have been poor," said the young minister at her graveside, "but her soul was rich. I stand humbly before her, for she was greater than I. She bore in her body the marks of the Lord Jesus. Never have *I* so suffered. Her life cries out against race hatred, race discrimination."

CHAPTER VII

The Family Goes West

For six unrewarding years the Pioneer and his pretty wife struggled on that stony Ontario farm, but, work as they would, strive as they might, they could not do more each year than pay the rent.

Rumours began to come in of that far away land out west, known as Manitoba. There, it was said, there were no stumps, no stones, no forests—all you had to do was put your plough in the sod and go for half a mile, or a mile, or as far as you thought you could pay for, and reward was yours the first year!

Albert listened to the whispers. He asked questions of returning neighbours, and he made up his mind. He was going west. Grandfather McCarty wept when he heard of the rash intentions of his long, gangling son, now a father of two children, with a third on the way. To go away out there into the unknown was to pass out of the world, the elder man felt, despite the fact that he himself had pioneered from Ireland at the age of twelve.

Sharing a settler's stock car with a neighbour, Albert and his meagre earthly possessions, in the spring of 1889, set out from Meaford for Carman, Manitoba, and after a week's slow travel, they reached their destination. A few farm implements, some household furniture, a pair of two-year-old Percheron colts and fifteen dollars in his pocket constituted the worldly wealth of the Pioneer.

He told his difficulties to the right parties, and with his fifteen dollars he bought a farm—a beautiful stretch of prairie land one hundred and sixty acres in extent, with not a hill nor a stump, and scarcely a stone to mar its table-level expanse.

He also bought lumber for a house, with his comical "capital," for credit was the order of the day at that time. Such faith had the town merchants in the bounty of the country, and in the industry of the incoming settlers that they readily staked a man coming in to make his start. Seldom were they let down.

The wife and three children—Rosalie, Roger and Margo—were to come two months later, the Pioneer told the lumber dealer. He must have a place to put them. Could he have enough lumber to build a shack 12 by 14 feet? There were sixty beautiful acres broken on the farm. He would have a crop on that and would be able to clear off his indebtedness in the fall.

"How much money have you got?" asked the lumber man.

"I had fifteen. Now I have only five left."

"Back up your wagon," said the benefactor, and forthwith piled on the greatly coveted boards.

"And here's your five dollars back," finished the dealer, when the load was complete. "Pay me when you grow the money."

Proudly Albert drove his prize of ninety dollars worth of lumber home, making his borrowed team walk just a little faster in his haste to exhibit his loot. He had lumber enough for a house 14 by 24; the dealer having scoffed at the idea of putting his family in a shack 12 by 14. Even at that there was no lumber to spare. Studding was set up four feet apart, and well does Margo remember how the swaying home had to be propped up with long timbers when one of those hefty Manitoba gales came along.

Anyway the house was built. True, it had only one layer of shiplap and one of thin siding to stand between the family and the weather, but winter was a long way off, and everything would be provided when that crop came in!

41

The weather had been very dry—so dry that there had been a meeting called in the little schoolhouse church for prayer for rain.

The day the wife and her three bairns arrived the morning dawned bright and clear as usual. But as the family neared home in the neighbour's open "democrat" a very black cloud appeared. When within a mile of their destination the clouds broke and a deluge ensued.

Parents and babies were soaked to the skin; and because the house was surrounded by white clay, dug from the cellar, a quagmire of mud all about the dwelling greeted the new arrivals. Mother and children had to be carried across the mire into the new home.

Mother forthwith got her first taste of Manitoba mud— famous to all who know it; for before Father and his helpers had got all the family and baggage into the house the scowload of clay attaching itself to each foot had covered the floor in a slimy mess, and it took the hoe to get it out and reveal the new bare floor.

Such a homecoming happily struck the young wife in her funnybone, and she just sat down and laughed. This was something to write home about!

The big thing was to get the crop in. All the motive power on the place was the team of two-year-old colts. And the colts were not even broken.

But the cows brought that matter to a head. They failed to come home one night, and the prairies were limitless. To start out on foot to find them was a formidable task. The colts must do the job.

Dappled grey they were, and as "pretty as a picture," the Pioneer always recalled. Albert had raised them himself and loved them dearly. Now he himself put their first harness on them, and hitched them to the buggy, starting them out across a ploughed field. They could not run very fast in this heavy footing, Albert thought.

But run they did. As soon as they saw the buggy coming

after them they jumped into their collars and away they went. Dirt flew in the face of the driver till he could scarcely see whither he was heading. The heavy field held down the pace of the terrified animals to a great extent, and their speed soon slackened from sheer exhaustion. By the time they had reached the ditch at the other end of the section they were under control.

Once across the ditch they refused to go a step further. Anything was better than having that awful rig bouncing after them, keeping right up with them no matter how fast they went.

It took coaxing and persuasion to get them moving again, when there was another uncontrollable race.

However, by the time they had got home they were "broke," docile and obedient. And they found the cows there before them!

From that day Nell and Prince were the work horses of the farm.

They put in the crop that spring on the sixty inviting acres, despite all the dire predictions of well-meaning neighbours. They harrowed and packed, as well as drawing the seeder; and with their driver resting them at the end of each mile round, and in the middle, they did the job.

Albert had no hay for them, and no oats. The best he could do was to get up at four o'clock each morning and turn them out on the luscious prairie, hobbled so that they could be readily caught again a couple of hours later when they must start their day's work. That they thrived and kept "fat as butter," was the Pioneer's boast. Prince and Nell that first year came through with flying colours, giving the young farmer his start and injuring themselves not at all.

"All I have had I owe to those colts," was ever the Pioneer's boast in subsequent and more prosperous years. The writer remembers them as the most loved team on the place. Although they lost their iron grey dapples in later years and turned snowy white, they never lost their youthful vigour up to their seventeenth year—the time when all the family bade them an affectionate farewell.

Because they were too old then to be brought to Alberta when the household moved to newer fields, they were superannuated with a brother farmer in Manitoba where they lived happily until they were twenty-six. Then a famine of feed struck the district and "John" mercifully took the faithful pair to the bush and gently chloroformed them into the happy hunting ground. Albert could not do it, nor otherwise dispose of his faithful pals when he left Manitoba, but all the family were satisfied when it was learned the "colts" had gone so gracefully from this world of toil.

A well was dug after a water witch had given the farmer a "bum steer." The first hole having been dug to a dry conclusion at the behest of the witch man, the second test was made with an auger to a depth of twelve feet, and a lovely spring of water was found. There was no lumber for cribbing, so Albert cut poplar poles from the near-by bush, putting first the small end down, then the big end of the pole, thus making quite a tight cribbing.

True, the water tasted a bit bitter for some time, and it acted like cascara when they drank it; but all that was remedied as the poplar sap was finally drained from the bark.

The first barn was of poles; the second of sod. The latter was much the warmer, even though straw was thrown over the first pole shed.

The crop was all that could be desired. Thirty bushels an acre it went, and the price was sixty-four cents a bushel. There was enough from the crop to pay all harvesting expenses, clear up the store bill and pay for the lumber! Of course there wasn't anything left to live on, but the stores trusted the beginners again until the next harvest.

In sixteen years of farming in Manitoba these pioneers only lost one crop. Thus the climb to independence was steady and sure. Then, of course, there was the little matter of paying for the farm. As the creditor began to press for his money, a lawyer was visited in the nearby town and through him a loan was raised which cleared off the whole indebtedness. This mortgage was easily met in succeeding years.

A book could be written reporting all the little joys and tragedies of these prairie pioneers, just as there could be about each and all the early settlers who made their way from poverty to prosperity on the cold but lucrative plains of Manitoba.

There were icy trips to "the hill" for wood for winter. These poles made fuel to keep the interior warm while exteriors raged with blizzards or froze under clear forty-below weather.

Many a long night of worry was involved, when Father did not come home through the blizzard.

"He won't try to make it in this storm," someone would say.

"I don't know," Mother would proffer; "Father doesn't like to stay away from home if he can help it."

Almost always out of the howl of the wind would come a faint tinkling of bells, growing more sure as the tired, yet eager, team, ploughed their way through the drifts homeward to warmth and shelter.

Out of the swirling mass of blinding whiteness, penetrable only a few feet at times, would finally emerge Father, sitting a-top his load, or walking ahead of the team, icicles hanging from his moustache, his huge fur collar white with frozen breath, icicles hanging from the lips of the tired horses, which had made the round trip of forty-four miles to the Pembinas that day between 4 A.M. and 9 P.M., allowing only time for the farmer feverishly to cut his load of poles and get going again. His only lunch would be his sandwiches which he had brought from home, and they ofttimes froze in his pocket before he could get around to eating them.

Strong and fearless the men had to be in those days. Equally courageous were the women.

There was the time, for example, when the roof of the precious McCarty house caught fire, and Mother was there

alone with the children. Timid to a fault, Mother nevertheless climbed up on that roof, right to the peak, with pails of
water, and put out the blaze.

There were incidents to write home about such as the
time Watch, the old yellow collie, ran away with four-year-
old Rosie on the hand sleigh.

Rosie, the eldest of the family and the pride and joy of all
concerned by reason of her head of yellow curls, her big
brown eyes and her ability to sing all the hymns her elders
knew almost before she could talk, was the special pal of old
Watch. He took great pleasure in drawing her about on the
hand sleigh.

But he was also a good wolfer; so when one day a lean
prairie wolf (the didn't call them coyotes in Manitoba)
appeared on the horizon just when Rosie was enjoying one
of her sunny day rides, Watch naturally forgot every other
responsibility and tore off across the field in the wake of the
wolf.

A tearful Rosie was picked up out of the snow not so far
from her home, but Watch disappeared entirely. Night came
and still he did not return.

A search found him fast in the "bluff," as the hedge of
small trees bordering the river was called. His harness had
become entangled in the limbs, and there he was, a sad and
dejected hunter.

There was the tragic time when Rosie disappeared from
circulation to be later found sitting under a currant bush
with most of her charming yellow curls adroitly cut off and
lying in a silken fluff all about her. The job of cutting one's
own hair at four years old is not considered easy, but this
young lady had managed it.

Settlers could not be weaklings in that pioneer period.
They had to take life as it came—cold, hot, windy, stormy,
dusty—but Nature offered them compensations as well as
trials. Glorious sunrises, blazing sunsets, star-filled nights,
long evenings of books when the family all gathered around

the big dining-table with the night lamp in the centre, and read themselves, either individually or collectively, into other worlds. Books were scarce, but neighbours were kind, and if a good book came into the neighbourhood it went the rounds, being loaned from one house to another.

There were wonderful concerts in the near-by church, and Christmas trees, at which the girls in their best blue and pink hair ribbons, and the boys in their best home-made pants, got up and did their stuff on the terrifying platform, and parents fairly burst with pride at the ability and beauty of their offspring.

A strenuous life, but not devoid of reward, was that lived by the early Manitoba farmer, and to those who played the game fairly and tirelessly steady progress provided compensation.

CHAPTER VIII

Manitoba Blizzards

anitoba has always been famous for its blizzards. No other province could apparently stir up such a relentless, death-dealing three-day rumpus as could this central province with its wide flat plains and its low temperatures.

Many lives have been lost in the merciless sweep of those winter gales, and stories of individual tragedies from blizzards were household knowledge among the early settlers.

Men were lost going from house to barn. Records tell of men, women or children freezing to death while within a few hundred yards of their own homes, the blinding snow making vision beyond a few feet impossible.

The village hotels had a good deal to do with such tragedies, as a few shots at the public bar made men just drowsy enough by the time they had driven or walked for even a short time through the hurricane to make them yield to the temptation common under such circumstances to lie down in the snow and enjoy that blissful sleep which alcohol promised.

There was the case of Freddie Goss. Freddie was an oddity in the community, as each new family in the neighbourhood soon discovered, to be ridiculed or pitied according to one's nature.

He had no feet, no hands, no lips and little nose. All had been frozen off the night he imbibed a little cheer at the

Carman bar, then went out to lie down in the lovely white snow to enjoy an undisturbed sleep.

Someone found him, and took him to hospital before he was quite dead.

His legs had to be amputated just below the knees, his fingers were all gone on one hand and the other arm had to come off just above the wrist.

With lips and nose missing, he was indeed a pitiful sight.

He had to earn his own living, as there was no relief for unfortunates in those days, and he did it by herding cattle. He learned to overcome the difficulty of mounting his pony by taking a run on his wooden pegs at her, and managing to throw himself over her low back and hence scramble on.

Everybody knew him and accepted him as a community fixture.

It was in church one peaceful Sunday morning that his disabilities created a disturbance—church was such a solemn place that any occurrence was talked about for long days after.

Freddie this morning was seated behind Mrs. Wilks. She was a stout old woman, always wearing her best black silk cape in the summer time; and this was summer time.

The cape had slipped off one shoulder, and Freddie gallantly thought to come to her aid. Clasping the edge of the collar between his two nude stubs he pushed it over her shoulder for her convenience.

She saw these handless arms coming and let out a shriek. What such a yell could do to a peaceful Sabbath morning sermon only those who have personal knowledge of such matters can appreciate.

There was the case of John Fox, the man who had a pair of six-year-old twins and who had just acquired another little daughter.

To keep his farm going and pay the winter grocery bills he was working in a nearby mill for the winter. Weather permitting, he walked home every week-end to visit his family. He had been home last week-end when Mother had gone to bed. With the aid of a good neighbour she had given birth to a nice little girl. Doctors were a superfluity in pioneer days. Even if there was one within ten miles he usually got there after the baby was born, anyway, so many did not trouble to call him.

When John set out next week on the five-mile hike home the weather looked very bad. Before he had gone far he found himself in the midst of a howling blizzard.

He got along fairly well the first of the trek. Although the road was full of drifts and the going very heavy, he managed to stay on the trail until he came to his own corner. The last half mile he had to swing off on his private road, which scarcely could be called a trail even at best.

The storm was getting fiercer every minute. Snow was frozen on his whiskers and banked upon his muffler. Snow on his eyelashes made it increasingly difficult for him to see anything. All was a swirling mass of whiteness, with the wind taking his breath away and the frost nipping at his toes and fingers. He kept his face covered with his mitts, applying snow once in a while to thaw out frostbites on cheek or nose.

Then he realized he was lost. All semblance of the trail had gone. North—south—east—west—it was all alike. There was nothing but that blinding density, all directions looking exactly the same.

That is the sensation that strikes terror in the heart of a man. One can travel in quite the opposite direction he wishes to take, or, more likely, he will revolve around in a circle until he is exhausted, and finally, yielding to the overwhelming impulse, will sink down in the snow—"just for a few minutes to rest," and that is the end. A delicious drowsiness creeps in, and after the storm is over someone finds the victim and another death by freezing goes on record.

It was only the thought of the little baby that kept John on his feet. There was no one but the six-year-old twins at home to feed the stock and care for mother and the child.

They might even be finding it impossible to get to the wood pile in this weather. They needed him, he felt sure. That little baby needed him. He pictured it shivering to death in a frigid house, or mother struggling out of bed to go hunt and find little Jimmie, bravely trying to make his way in from the barn.

A plainsman knows that when he is lost he is lost. There is little use in trying to follow your instincts and go this way or that. You are just about sure to come back to the place you started. So when John came across a fallen tree he accepted that as his friend for the night. He walked up and down beside it, tramping a path for himself, which path would almost be obliterated by the time he traversed it back again.

It was exhausting. It was overwhelming. To make matters worse, he had no supper. Having told the cook he was going home that evening, no place was set for him when supper was called, and so he had left on an empty stomach.

If he had only had a good hot meal in him before he had left he felt he could bear this thing better.

Up and down, back and forth, with the storm howling in his ears, snow in his eyes, snow in his nostrils, his feet numb, his arms swinging in continual beat against his body as he slapped them against himself to beat warmth into his chilling frame.

He knew this fallen tree. It was only a quarter of a mile from his home. Yet he dared not leave it. He must tramp, and keep tramping.

Mother was not worrying about dad. She thought he would surely not have started before the storm broke, and she and the twins were getting along all right. Jimmie had piled in plenty of wood, and little Sue had got the batch of bread safely in the oven and baked to a turn.

Little Sue—who had only been two and a half pounds when she was born was still a tiny mite. She had had to stand on a box beside her mother's bed while she followed the sick woman's directions about mixing the precious batter. The bread pan on a chair beside the bed, the mother directed first the water to a certain depth, then the flour. Little Sue had quite a time to stir this mixture, the spoon being bigger than her arm, but with the home-made hop yeast and salt added, the batter was ready to be dragged back beside the stove where it was carefully covered with the red cotton table cloth especially reserved for this use.

Sue's loaves were not quite so symmetrical as her mother's, but with mother encouraging her from the bed she had managed to knead and roll the loaves until the pan was full, and then to bake the whole. It was all quite a job for such a midget, but she had to be hands and feet for mother for everything these days.

The wind howled and raged outside, and there was such thick frost on the panes that it took a long time to melt a hole in the cold whiteness to get a peep at the outside world.

There was nothing to see anyway, but a solid mass of obscurity.

Jimmie had not attempted to go out to do the chores that night, Old Buck, the horse, and Jack, the ox, and Peggy, the cow, were going to be pretty thirsty but that was better than having a lost boy, mother ruled. Anyway, the barn pump was frozen solid and no water could be got from it until a long thawing process took place next morning.

Yes, they did need father very badly, but then of course he could not get home in this storm.

When day broke next morning there was a slight lessening of the gale. Mother was just thinking she would soon have to call Jimmie again (he had been up several times during the night to pile wood in the stove) when she heard a frightening sound. It sounded as though someone had tumbled into the circle of snow which now banked the door to the eaves and had bumped into the front door. Sue and Jimmie, both aroused by mother's calls, came shivering in their flannelette nighties.

"Open the door," directed mother, her face as fearful as that of her children. This might be anything.

In tumbled—father!

There he lay, a huddled heap of unconsciousness on the door mat, snow and ice covering him from head to foot, icicles hanging from his moustache.

Managing to pull him inside so that the door might be closed to shut out the icy blast that immediately filled the room with steam, the children stood over him, sobbing. Mother wept at her helplessness, but gave directions. Father revived speedily. He was not frozen, merely utterly exhausted, and quite numb all over from the cold.

Naturally, all soon was joy and relief in the little log house. Father had kisses of gratitude for the baby and her mother, and for his two brave children who had measured up so well to meet the emergencies of the storm. Gladness such as only deliverance from danger brings reigned that day in the storm-swept cabin.

Manitoba people are courageous people, it is averred. Brought up from childhood to face such rigours could they be anything else?

Then there was the true tale of the district that lost its pretty young school teacher in a prairie blizzard.

That took place in the hilly country west of the Pioneer's home, where there was brush and even some trees.

There were just eleven scholars in the school, and they adored their petite little instructress. So did all the bachelors in the neighbourhood. Particularly did Hans Nelson. He was tall, and fair, and very fine looking; and he had one of the coziest little homes in the neighbourhood, even boasting indoor water. Built against a hillside down which tumbled a brook of clear pure water from a gurgling spring, he had gouged out a deep basin and trapped himself a year-round supply.

Even such an inducement as this got him exactly nowhere. Miss Dale (Alice, Hans called her in his heart) was not marrying any farmer, particularly a Manitoba farmer.

To endure a season in the country until she earned enough to go to college was all that she could stand.

Then that blizzard came along.

It was a bad one, striking in the early afternoon with such fury that parents did not have time to hook up their bob sleighs and go after their children. Usually storms gave enough warning to enable wise fathers to get out their boxed sleighs and hasten to school. All lined up, one outfit after another, the teams would plow home through the storm, the children covered up in the bottom of the "bob" or carryall, while "father" drove, sitting sideways to the wind, protecting his cheek against the stinging snow that cut like sharp pebbles, urging the horses on against the wind. Their noses suffered, too, and they strained in their collars to drag their load through the big drifts, sometimes belly-deep.

Drivers would lose sight of the team following behind, and would shout above the gale—

"Are you coming?"

A hoo-hoo through the storm would give assurance, and the caravan of nondescript sleighs would continue until each branched to his particular road and each took a chance on making it alone.

This time the storm broke too suddenly for fathers to get on the road. They had told the teacher that in any such emergency she was to stay at the school all night, keeping the children with her.

This order was being carried out. Long cord wood had been piled in to suffice for the night, and most of the children were in high glee at the thought of this adventure. True there were only a few slices of bread left in dinner pails, and thoughts of the hot potatoes and the fried pork at home made some feel very homesick, but the school as a whole had not had time to get to the teary stage before sleigh bells were heard coming through the storm.

It was Hans. His big bob-sleigh drew up at the door; his fine team puffing and blinking in the wind. He had blankets enough for all, and he had come to take teacher and the whole school home to his place. He lived a mile away, half of the distance being through brush, where the fury of the gale was tempered.

He left a note at the school telling what he was about to do, in case some courageous father should manage to fight his way to the schoolhouse. This was a grand adventure to the older children, and with encouragement from Teacher, even the younger ones forgot that mother was going to be worrying about them all night, and went willingly along.

For three days the storm raged. The boys shovelled snow to keep the path open to the barn. They split wood. The girls and Teacher found everything to work with in the house, and what good meals they had! If there were a few homesick tears when night time came, Teacher and Hans told them so many stories and organized such funny games that even the most lonely was comforted.

They slept on the floor, under robes and coats. It was Teacher and Hans who, unselfishly, volunteered to sit by the fire and keep it going. A sleepy eye, opened occasionally, found them earnestly engaged in conversation. They seemed to be interested in the same book and appeared to have much to talk about. Before relieved fathers, redirected by the note at the schoolhouse, had come to claim their offspring, when the blow had abated, Nellie Pearce, the oldest young miss of the school, had said knowingly—

"Hans is sweet on Teacher!"

And that is the Pioneer's report of how Westbluff lost its pretty schoolmarm in a blizzard.

CHAPTER IX

Dick, the Sky Pilot

ick was a young theological student—one of the many sent out to The West to try their hands at missionary work, or, as was often the case, sent as recruits to the harvest fields in the autumn that they might earn some wherewithal to carry them through another year of college, on their long journey to ministerial ordination.

Dick belonged to the latter classification. He hailed from Winnipeg and, from sheer necessity, migrated annually to the country in quest of a stake.

This year he had come to the farm of old Bill Smith whose half section adjoined the McCarty place. Bill was a hard-fisted man, successful but at a price. He bullied his way through everything to financial rewards; all obstacles in his path going down before his iron will, regardless of who was hurt in the process.

Before leaving home Dick Slater's mother had told him—"Now lad, don't forget to let your light shine." In his new environment Dick was finding it pretty tough to stand on his feet at all, let alone do any light broadcasting in such a darkened atmosphere.

Mrs. Smith was a woman whose shell seemed impenetrable. She moved about her work with quiet efficiency without a word to anyone. She sat stiffly at table paying no heed to Bill's rough talk and coarse jests. Smith himself was immediately put down in Dick's mind as "impossible."

The bright spot in the household was Kelsie.

Kelsie was fifteen, small and petite, compressed into non-talkativeness like her mother. Her clear blue eyes had gone over him appraisingly when he came, but her greeting had been most aloof and apparently disinterested. He felt, however, that her shell was much more vulnerable than that of her mother's and he was not averse to finding out, when the opportunity should offer.

There was little time for anything but work at Bill Smith's, however. Five a.m. saw all hands turning out, including the two Polish men who were doing the stooking and helping with the chores along with himself and Bill.

At six o'clock all sat down to a farm breakfast, porridge, potatoes and fried pork, dried fruit sauce, and tea and toast constituting the usual programme. Farm hands had to be fed if you expected to get work out of them.

The Polish men were slight of build and were only of medium height, yet the way they could toss the sheaves into the stooks all day long, walking silently from one windrow to another, filled Dick with admiration.

"That's all they knew in their own country—work and trouble," Bill had proffered when Dick commented on their tireless gait. "They say they were persecuted by the Armenians—just got out alive. So they appreciate a chance to earn a livin' here, even if they have to work for it. Not like you city fellers—never knew what hard work wuz till you growed up, and then not relishin' finding out. Yep, for a good worker give me one of them downtrodden Europeans every time."

Dick had been assigned a job on the second binder after old Bill had taken one look at him.

"Those white hands of yours and them pink cheeks mean just one thing—you're soft."

Dick's mechanical ability had increased his rating on the farm, and Bill soon learned to turn Dick loose on the job when his binder refused to tie or the reel jammed.

It was the first day out that Dick scored a point with Bill on this count. Sheaves were being kicked out on the bundle carrier not bound and Bill had exercised all the profanity and mechanical knowledge he could muster, all in vain. He was just threatening to take a sledgehammer to the reaper and smash the d——d thing when Dick came to the rescue. A simple adjustment did the trick.

"I never knew a parson that was any good before—for anything but tellin' other folks what to do," Bill had rasped. "Guess you haven't been a parson long enough to get spoiled."

Dick had clashed with Bill the third day after his arrival on this religion business. He had asked if he might say grace at the table.

He had been brought up that way. He didn't enjoy his meals without it.

Old Bill snorted.

"None of that tom-foolery around here," he had decreed. Unexpectedly it was Mrs. Smith who came to the rescue.

She stepped out of the pantry with the first decisive utterance Dick had heard her make since his arrival.

"He's going to say it if he likes," she snapped. "You've had your way round here long enough, Bill Smith!"

"Blow me down," Bill pondered. "Well, shoot the works, boy. But make it snappy. Wheat shelling out five bushels to the acre."

When Dick had raised his eyes after his few words of thanksgiving they opened to meet Kelsie's. She was regarding him intently, and she blushed vividly as their eyes met. What did that mean? Dick wondered. One never knew what went on in the mind of a girl, leastwise this silent, intense little girl.

Because it was holiday time Kelsie was her mother's right hand helper. Kelsie liked to cook, and was always springing some new dish out of the *Family Herald* cookery corner on them. The rest of the housework she abhorred, but did it because somebody had to do it. Her mother was worked to death—endless lines of washing for family and men, endless loaves of bread to be baked, mountains of ironing, butter to be churned and moulded, milk to care for night and morning, floors to wash, beds to make—there was no end whatever to the round of labour that beset these farm women.

It was whispered that Mrs. Smith had eloped with Bill from Ontario when she was but sixteen, to get away from a domineering father, and that she had only succeeded in getting out of the frying pan into the fire.

Perhaps that was why she was so tight lipped. Having made a bad deal she was too proud to squawk about it. She was just putting up with it with the least fuss possible.

That she loosened up when she was alone with Kelsie Dick felt sure, for he had caught them chuckling together over a scrap of paper. They had hastily put it away on his appearance. It was not until weeks later that Dick learned it was one of Kelsie's poems, and it was about her father. "Cock o' the Barnyard," had been the title.

"No, you can't see it," Mrs. Smith had said to Dick. "Kelsie shouldn't write such things."

Dick knew that such a topic had its possibilities and was aware that more than caricaturing poems could be written about old Bill. The temper of the man tried him sorely. He could stand being bawled out himself when he hadn't deserved it, but it was mighty hard to stand by and see Bill abuse the animals.

"He needs a change of heart," Dick told himself, but such a possibility seemed very remote.

There was that very dramatic day when Bill, on the rampage as usual over everything and everybody, had unhitched his horses from the binder and forgot one trace.

A runaway seemed imminent, for there was a bronco among the quartette. Only the fact that Dick was there and strong enough to throw his weight into holding the animals prevented an immediate wild break such as is the dread of every farm.

When some semblance of order was restored, instead of being grateful, Bill, still in a rage, sought only to vent his temper on the frightened animals.

He seized the piece of trace and set about beating the offending bronco. That was too much for a horse but recently captured from the range of Alberta.

Pinto bolted, taking the other three with him.

Away they went across the stubble, between windrows, over stooks, dirt flying behind fleeing hoofs in a dusty cloud, a wild sight, a fearsome spectacle.

Runaway horses gather up a terror in themselves that is unexplainable. With all control gone, they seem to be afraid of their unchecked liberty, and follow their primitive instinct just to flee.

They were heading straight for the pasture, and the pasture was fenced. If they ran into that barbed wire something was going to happen. Old Bill watched them, forgetting even to curse.

It was Dick who found his voice.

"You're full of the devil, Bill Smith," he cried. "See what you've done. You're full of the devil!"

The horses were surely not going to slam into that fence! They did just that! They hit it four abreast.

The posts went down before the impact like nine pins, and the team went through, stumbling a bit as the wires broke.

Bill Smith groaned.

"They'll be all tore to pieces in front," he mumbled, covering his eyes.

Dick knew he was right. No team could go through a three-strand barbed wire fence without wounds.

From then on the runaways circled the pasture. Their speed was diminishing, and Pinto, the bronco, seemed to be lagging greatly. Dick and Bill were now running after them, but it was Fred and Jacob, the Polish men, who reached the horses first.

Panting, sweating, exhausted, bleeding, the horses had come to a halt in front of the further fence. They stood shaking and gasping as Fred and Jacob got control of the dragging lines and held them securely.

What a sight!

All were scratched and cut; but it was Pinto who had hit the wire first, and had paid the price.

His whole breast lay open in a foot-long gash of raw meat laid bare between his front legs.

Dick was angry, but he took charge. He drove the trembling animals to the barn and carefully took off their harness. He got the Polish men to fetch water and they bathed the more serious wounds.

There was old Jake, of whom Bill was really fond, with his knee cap torn open while a cut artery in Flossie's side demanded immediate attention. It spurted blood at every heart beat.

Dick knew a little about first aid. He gave orders, and the men obeyed. One after the other all the animals were treated but Pinto. He looked hopeless.

"What do you want to do with him, Boss?" Dick asked as the men stood in the box stall and inspected the grievous wound.

"Looks like he's only good for to be taken out and shot. And he was gettin' to be a good horse, too."

"I believe it's worth trying," Dick said, as if to himself. "Fetch me the strings off your violin, Bill. Get Kelsie to sterilize them. She knows how. I saw it in her home nursing book."

Kelsie brought the surgical implements herself—a dish of boiled water, a darning needle, and sterilized violin strings.

The chastened Pinto was standing with front feet braced, motionless, taking no alarm even at Kelsie's entrance. He was too dazed and confused for ordinary emotion.

Kelsie acted as nurse while Dick performed his operation. Stitch after stitch went into the gaping wound, Pinto never budging. Pain had numbed the prick of the needle and draw of the gut string.

Pale, refusing to look, Kelsie stood with her dish of water while Dick finished his job.

Old Bill, unable to stand it, had fled to the pump. It was time to fill the trough, and he recuperated his failing strength on the heavy handle.

"Full of the devil, full of the devil," the pump seemed to say as the handle went up and down. A whole afternoon lost, one horse put out of commission for the season, if not for good, the other three impaired. Bill for once was ashamed of himself.

"You'd make a good nurse," Dick encouraged, noting Kelsie's pale cheeks.

"Not very," breathed the impromptu assistant, her knees weakening; and so it was Dick's privilege to play the part of the strong man in helping a staggering girl out to the fresh air.

"You can do a lot of things," Kelsie applauded when she had got her breath. "I'm—I'm glad you came here. I hope you stay a while."

And taking herself in hand she walked erectly to the house.

The operation was a success. Situated as the deep wound was, between the front legs, there was little to disturb it, and it healed in due course.

Daily, Kelsie and Dick became better friends. She even let him look into her precious composition book.

"Not even Teacher was allowed to see these," she told Dick as she brought down her holy of holies. It was filled with little verses, written by herself, some crude, some remarkably mature, all voicing a great appreciation for Nature and an impatience with the mundane things of life.

"There's something so swell about life," she confided to Dick; "the sunrises, the sunsets, the moonlight—that harvest feeling—don't they make you feel so big inside, and yet so little. Don't they make you feel like life is something to be thankful for. And then comes dishwashing, and dirty floors, and Dad's curses, and wash day—and all those things that go with this farm. I'll bet life is different in the city. I want to go to the city."

"Life in the city has its squalor, too," Dick had told her. "It has its heartbreaks and its loneliness. I guess happiness isn't just in any particular place. I guess happiness is something you have to find inside of you, just where you are."

"But it's harder on the farm," Kelsie insisted. "Look at Mother. She used to write poetry too. Now look at her. All washed out. Twenty years of manure tracks on the floor, twenty years of dirty milk pails, twenty years of nothing but work, work, and more work. I want to go to college and be something besides a farm drudge."

"The farm could be all right, Kelsie, if people didn't let the light go out of things. Nothing is any good unless you have that light inside of you that reflects on all about you. Then everything is all right wherever you are."

Dick was thinking of his mother and her farewell instructions.

It was after harvest was all over that Dick said one evening, "I'll be going back to college, soon, Kelsie. Guess your dad will be glad to see the last of me. He doesn't talk much to me ever since that runaway day."

"He's been different," Kelsie reflected. "He's been a lot tamer. Guess that day made him ashamed of himself. I believe you've done him good. Do you know, I almost believe he'd send me to college when you go if you'd ask him—" this last with breathless daring.

"Kelsie!" the idea very evidently was fraught with unalloyed delight for young Dick.

It was in the barn that Dick sought out old Bill.

"Yes, she's hinted at it afore," Bill admitted. "An' I don't know but what it mightn't hurt her any. I've been a'thinkin' that if college didn't do her any more harm than it's done you, perhaps it wouldn't hurt to send her for a spell. You know—I ought to fire you and not pay you any wages—after what you said to me—about me havin' a devil. But do you know I believe maybe you wuz right. Believe I have had a little of Beelzebub in me. I've been doin' a lot of thinkin' lately. One of these days you may find me a changed man, lad."

The evident sincerity of rough Bill surprised and touched Dick.

"I'm glad, sir," he said simply.

"An'," as Bill reached for the curry comb and set to work on the now tame Pinto. "We've had a mighty fine crop this year. I've got a nice little egg in the bank. If Kelsie wants to go to that college of yours you can tell her it's all right by me. Guess it'll cost a heap, but then maybe I might as well spend it that way as any other."

Dick's eyes were glowing.

"An'," as he ran carefully over the now healed wound in Pinto's breast—"When you get her all educated up if you think she'll make a good preacher's wife, you can marry her."

CHAPTER X

Echoes From
the Barr Colony

T wo years before the McCartys left Manitoba on their ever-westward trek, something of interest transpired in the Northwest Territories, as Alberta and Saskatchewan were still called. Faint echoes concerning the Barr colonization scheme had reached their ears, and now, in the newly formed Province of Alberta, still further rumours regarding the establishment of the big Barr colony on the border of the provinces were in circulation.

Horses were being rounded up on the ranges in Southern Alberta for sale to these new settlers, and ranchers and punchers saw their horses depart for this Colony destination with many misgivings and some jovial anticipation. Visions of what was going to happen to would-be farmers, with settlers green from the cities of England endeavouring to farm with these wild outlaws or even half-broken broncos, came to mind, making for hilarious conjecture among the unfeeling and for real pity among the more humane.

The Pioneer relates the experiences of young Willy Weaver who, with his family, was a member of the Colony. It was in 1903 that Rev. Isaac Barr of the Imperial Canadian Army conceived the idea of importing a whole colony of settlers at once from the Old Land, and forthwith he made arrangements with the Dominion Lands Department and with immigration authorities in Canada for a sizable tract of prairie in the untouched prairie wilderness half way between the towns of Saskatoon and Edmonton. Then he opened an office in London and proceeded to book up his settlers. They were to have 160 acres of homestead land for the price of $10, the holding to be theirs after three years of settlement and development, according to homestead rules.

It was his advertisement for certain key people which attracted the attention of young Will's father, a baker who had been told that his calling was unhealthy for him. If he could escape to the open spaces, even under guise of his profession, he could ultimately, he felt, be released to become one of the agriculturists which ambition these three thousand migrating pilgrims expected to realize. The outcome was that Mr. Barr hired the whole Weaver family—mother, father, two sons and a daughter. Will was seventeen and a half, and his father had to buy his release from the army before he could go along with the party on this alluring adventure.

"We left on March 4, 1903," said Willy. "It took us thirteen days to cross the Atlantic. Halifax gave us our first taste of what we might expect in Canada. There snow was piled so high along the sidewalks that we could not see the horse-drawn street cars which we could hear lurching along on the other side of the white barricades.

"Saskatoon, our railway terminus, we found to be a town of 113 inhabitants. We were with the second advance guard, about fifty travellers having already reached Saskatoon with the initial contingent, to set up tents for themselves and us. Now it was our task to raise a city of canvas homes extensive enough to accommodate the three thousand who were due to arrive in about ten days."

The tent city was erected on the north side of the railway tracks, where the heart of the city now is, and a huge marquee tent, provided by the federal government in which to serve meals to those not immediately equipped with housekeeping facilities, was filled with tables and benches sufficient to seat 250 at once. Frederick Weaver had been engaged as caterer for this great dining-room, with all the family as assistants. To young Willy and his brother fell the lot of dishwashing; a chore from which they escaped to other pursuits just as soon as it was humanly possible.

Before leaving London the emigrants had been invited to invest in the Barr Colony Co-operative Society. Such monies were to purchase supplies for the marquee, the investors were told, and they would later receive dividends in addition to having their immediate needs supplies. The Weavers put in £25, then evaluated at nearly $125, but Willy said that all that his parents ever had returned to them was a box of thread. Those who had invested more, of course, fared worse.

It was after the Colony was safely established under canvas, ready for their first big push across the open prairie to their final destination, 180 miles distant, that Jim Barr, brother of Leader Isaac Barr, came into the picture. Seeing his opportunity to make a clean-up here, he shipped in several carloads of wild horses, mostly from Montana, and proceeded to sell them to the newcomers as farm animals. Covered wagons were simultaneously imported by one of the established machinery firms of that time, and Jim's task was to persuade the immigrants that his horses were all that was needed to make them real westerners, ready for the trek to their new homes.

His prices ranged from $60 a team to $300, and most of these animals had never had a harness on them. True, he had a camp of cowboys at hand who assayed to break the critters, but most of the horses as turned over to the unknowing newcomers were still decidedly in the raw. What casualties resulted form the attempts of these inexperienced Englishmen to even get a harness on their bucking backs, only those who were there can report. One case is cited of a purchaser who paid $125 for a buckskin mare—Meg by name—who remained in his possession just one day. Going to get her in the morning, after a night of being staked out, he found stakes and mare missing. Meg was never again seen in those parts. This case was repeated many times over among the would-be farmers, as well as other disasters, such as runaways, injuries inflicted with teeth or heels to hapless drivers, and upsets.

It was during this period of wild-west upheavals that young Willy got to the end of his endurance in the dishwashing job. This was not his idea of life in the far West. Forthwith he applied to burly Jim Barr, later branded a reprobate, for a job, and soon, clad in woolly chaps, a broad cowboy hat and spurs, Willy the Westerner was sent out atop a little pony to help herd the horses. The band were taken out to feed in the morning and brought back to camp at night. Oxen, also, were being offered to the trekkers as means of travel, and these wild steers, just off the range, proved about as difficult to handle as were the horses.

However, despite all the problems encountered in getting started, small groups began to depart; their prairie schooners loaded with furniture and personal effects, bound for Battleford, their first stopping place, one hundred miles distant. Willy, eager to see the land of promise, secured his parents' permission to proceed ahead of them with a neighbouring pilgrim, a Josiah Buckleby who was a Sunday School superintendent back home, and with whom Willy would surely be in good hands.

About thirteen miles a day was all that the caravan would make, and such good time was marked up only when no mud holes were encountered. But every valley through which the long procession wound its way proved to be a Waterloo. As many as ten wagons would be stuck hub deep in the mud, with neighbour trying to pull out neighbour, and the whole company held up for hours before solid ground was again gained by all. The oxen did better in these bogs than the horses; their cloven hooves seeming to come loose from the mire better than did the round hoof of a horse. At Battleford another marquee had been set up, this centre serving as a half-way house for the trekkers. They now had their own tents, and they made what progress they could in the daytime, camping at night to rest weary bones in themselves and their animals.

Willy had not gone far on the trek before he began to be very fed up with his new guardian. Neither he nor the twenty-year-old son, Hector, was ever allowed to ride. The load of household effects and foodstuffs which filled the schooner was heavy enough, without any excess human weight. So for the full one hundred miles the boys plodded stolidly beside the wagon, their feet acquiring new blisters with every passing day, and their bodies ofttimes numb with the bitter north wind that swept across the bald prairie, even though it was now April. They walked on the lee side of the caravan, and Willy, in his ulster with its flapping cape and sleeveless body, remembers how he longed for even an hour in that pitching schooner, if for no other purpose than to get warm.

Finally, after what seemed an endless march, they came within sight of Battleford. The police barracks were here, as this was an operating centre for a huge section of territory for the red-coated mounties. When Willy was out walking the next day, a mountie rode by, and he stared, fascinated. The scarlet coat, the blue pants with their stripe, the broad hat, the fine mount, all did something to him, and he resolved right there that he was not going on to the Colony. He was going to join the Mounted Police. He wired back to Saskatoon to his parents for permission, and next day, with a pal named Arthur, presented himself at the barracks.

Willy gave his age as eighteen, and the two were accepted forthwith. They were sworn in as special constables, and their job was to circulate around among the tents to see what they could see. Silverware and other precious heirlooms had been brought from England by the women-folk of the invading army, and in some cases there was thieving for such articles going on. Remittance men, misfits and other questionable characters had been included in the three thousand, so that the new settlers were not, in all cases, the most desirable immigrants.

Full of their own importance and the dignity of their new office, the boys sought assiduously for culprits. The only rascals they were able to unearth, however, were some young men whom they heard plotting a raid on the tent in which the few young women who had come with the trekkers were housed. The boys were applauded for this possible crime-discovery, and Willy felt that he had started on his career as a wild-west policeman.

Approval from Saskatoon was duly forthcoming, and for the next three years the young English boy was part and parcel of the N.W.M.P. He was shortly transferred to Regina, where there were two hundred horses at the barracks' stables for him to handle and admire, and where he got an inkling of the barracks life as lived by these world-famous guardians of the plains. Willy was the camp bugler, and when trumpets were issued from Ottawa he learned, and taught others, all the calls belonging to the mounties.

"Indeed," he reported, "I'm the guy who taught the calls to each trumpeter in the six western divisions surrounding Regina. They came from Calgary and all about to take instructions from me in this line, which I had learned thoroughly in England."

"As for the Colony," concluded Willy, "most of them made good. Of course there were weaklings and ne'er-do-wells who would never make good anywhere, but when they recovered from the first shock of what lay ahead of them— the hardships, the poverty, the long fight to get a toe-hold—instead of the land of promise which they had been led to believe awaited them—they got down to brass tacks and made good pioneers.

"The city of Lloydminster today, surrounded by good homes and prosperous farms, despite numerous years of drought, hail, storm and other plagues, speaks for itself. Most of us English immigrants ultimately make real Canadians."

CHAPTER XI

Western Fever Again Strikes

T he McCarty family was in a dither. Indeed the whole neighbourhood of Clinton was in a dither, for was not Albert McCarty, after fourteen years' residence in this prosperous and flourishing Province of Manitoba, talking such sacrilege as moving?

Albert had been very successful. In the whole fourteen years of his sojourn in this hand-picked neighbourhood, he had really lost only one crop. That was a record for any community. His average yields had been among the best, for he was a good farmer. His house had increased in dimensions. He had water pumped into his kitchen from a huge cistern in the cellar. He had a piano. He had a fine layout of barns and plenty of livestock to fill them. He had five children; two, Ross and Chris, having been born in Manitoba. Most convincing of all, he had been able to send his two elder children to college in Winnipeg—an undertaking thought possible by very few in the district. On top of that, he continued to give liberally to the missionary fund.

Yes, Albert McCarty and his wife had done well in Manitoba. Why should they dream of leaving?

But Albert had heard a lecture on Alberta. A six-foot giant, ex-army, ex-adventurer, now promoter, had come into the district. Many lecturers came to Clinton. They made the circuit under the auspices of some branch of the church, or they came on their own, and their messages brought the isolated community glimpses of the outside world which kept the settlers better informed than their patronizing city cousins, just sixty miles away, deemed possible.

There were temperance lectures, reports from returned missionaries, travelling elocutionists, ever-recurring travelling evangelists, and occasionally such events as an Arctic explorer or a persecuted Armenian, relating the horrors of his experiences. Such stories were of Montana, or points further south, but here was a land in their own dominion that boasted stampedes, round-ups, corrals, lariats, wild horses—and cowboys!

So this is what the neighbourhood shortly heard: Albert McCarty—their Albert McCarty, superintendent of the Sunday School, leading tenor in the choir, loved neighbour and fixture in Clinton—had gone daft over Major Schoof's rosy pictures of another West, and he was going land-seeking in Alberta, and taking that tow-headed tomboy Margo with him.

Mother McCarty was mildly interested. Albert hadn't made a mistake yet about getting ahead, and he wouldn't be moving away from Clinton if it were not going to be for the better. And if Margo had managed to wangle a ticket out of him and was going along, that was her good luck. Father was a great calf anyway. It was just because at the last minute he got lonesome at the idea of going away off there by himself for a whole month that Margo had wrung that final "All right" from him a few days before he was to leave. Uncle Slade would stay with Mother and do the chores.

Although the thermometer registered forty below on the day of their departure, there was Grandpa among others at the station, all bundled up in his muffler and wearing his new Christmas mitts, to see them off. Grandpa and Grandma had long ago been transplanted from their Ontario hearthside to a comfortable frame house in the village of Sunnyside, five miles from Albert's farm, and they, like their adventuring son, had had to agree that Manitoba had its compensations for the ambitious which the older province could not offer. They were quite content to spend the rest of their declining years in Sunnyside.

"It's never satisfied you are, lad," came from the grizzled old veteran as he waited with his long son on the station platform. "Going away off to find another country, when you're doing so fine here. It's a restless spirit you have, to be sure."

"Well, I never made a get-away on a swinging gangplank against all the laws of the country," retorted his remembering son.

The inrush of the huge black engine, bell clanging, smoke belching, icicles hanging from every drip, and with the thundering coaches in tow, provided the first thrill of the journey. Margo had stood on this platform many times before, to watch the train come in. Half the town did likewise, and if they chanced to be in the village at train time, country shoppers often availed themselves of the privilege also. Three times a week the C.N.R. cavalcade snorted into this quiet little village and out again. This time they were going with it.

The trip into the wonderland of the West lasted a month, and, as Father had subconsciously hoped, young Margo not only kept him from getting homesick and turning back before he had half completed his circuit, but her delight at every new experience was contagious, adding to his own enjoyment of this, his first free and unfettered journey into a new country. The trip from Ontario had been made in a stock car. Now he and Margo travelled in luxurious plush, with all the world ahead of them as they pushed forward into the little-known last West.

They left Winnipeg, January 5, 1904, and their impressions of that journey, as reported to the home folk by Father, were of wide reaches of farm-dotted prairie, snow covered and cold, extending as far as the Manitoba border. Beyond that, in Saskatchewan, evidences of population became more intermittent; fences were fewer and farm buildings farther apart. Bitterly cold weather delayed their train for a whole day at one point, until frozen pipes in the engine could be thawed out.

Medicine Hat, their first stop, disclosed broad vistas of rolling hills, snowless and dotted with feeding cattle. They were now getting into the Chinook belt. Father was greatly impressed with the farming possibilities of Southern Alberta. Here cattle roamed the plains all winter, rustling their own feed. Yes, in severe winters the loss from exposure might be quite heavy, when whole herds would go over a cut bank in a storm, to perish at the foot of the cliff, or where animals died by the hundreds of starvation because they could not get at the grass under the snow; but then, what were a few hundred head among so many thousands!

Northern Alberta manifested too much scrub and brush to suit Father. Anyway, who wanted to go so far North? He did not know then that Strathcona and Edmonton, the twin cities marking the terminus of the railway, would in his lifetime be the jumping-off place for a great empire above and beyond these towns. To the prairie travellers, the mountains proved enthralling. Banff, wrapped in its silent blanket of spotless snow, rugged peaks towering above peace-filled valleys in majestic quiet, was to them awe-inspiring.

Vancouver, their ultimate destination, was to the land-seeking twain a joke. Who would want to live in a place where it rained all winter? And Lulu Island—the idea of paying $100 an acre for that dyke-girt, below-sea-level, so-called farming community, when whole sections waited the plow, treeless, stumpless, almost stoneless, back there in Alberta. Again, Albert McCarty did not foresee the day when land on this now-despised delta would be bringing $1500 or better an acre, and that he, himself, would be spending his last days in the shelter of its dykes.

It was in the town of Nanton, Alberta, on the McLeod-Calgary line, that Father finally bought up section after section of beautiful prairie land, some of it for $9 an acre, and some for $15, which he was to sell five years later, with improvements for as much as $40 an acre. Profiteering? Yes, so it could be called, but to Father McCarty and to other investors who got in on the ground floor of this boom, there seemed no wrong. To the one who had enterprise enough to move with the tide belonged the reward, and no doubt the man who came after would continue to make well on his investment. There was no limit to what Canada had to offer to one with vision and not afraid to work.

Thus it was that next spring saw the McCarty family again uprooted from their soil and transplanted from one fine province to a better—from the viewpoint of farmer opportunity and compensation. After a few months spent in a rented house in the village of Nanton, while their fine new home up there on the section bordering the township on the west was being completed, the McCartys were established in the huge frame house; first in this neighbourhood to be equipped with waterworks, electric light and a fireplace. Now they were ready for whatever this land of promise, fresh from the hand of Nature, had to offer. Unfurrowed, unfenced, dotted by buffalo wallows and badger holes, and cut deep with trails leading from south to north, from McLeod to Edmonton, from Saskatchewan to the Crow's Nest Pass; the deep ruts told the story of ox-carts, of covered wagons, of horsemen, cowboys and mounted police, and all the history which the past fifty years had written over the face of the prairie and which soon was to yield to another phase of western progress.

In his five short years of residence in Alberta, Albert McCarty proved, to the chagrin of the calamity prophesying cattlemen, that Southern Alberta was not too dry to grow wheat. His half-section of Red Fyfe, which yielded an average of 63.4 bushels to the acre, was photographed by real estate men, printed on calendars and dishes, and used as advertising matter to bring hundreds, and later thousands, into this endlessly expansive new country. Here plow and harrow were soon to displace cayuse and rider; seeder and binder to replace round-up and camp-fire, and the free range to be swallowed up in homestead and small holding of orthodox agriculturists.

Bitter was the transition to the vainly-protesting cattleman who, for long decades, had been able to pull his chuckwagon up beside some inviting stream and, from that beginning, claim all the surrounding land about him as his range. Small wonder that the invasion of the farmer was to him hard to accept, and many fights and feuds ensued before the free-holders were convinced that their day was ended.

CHAPTER XII

Light and Shadow
in Alberta

B arr Colony immigrants were not the only westerners, of course, who faced hardship and tribulation. The prairie was impartial in its dispensation of hard knocks, whether one lived in Manitoba or the Northwest Territories. Albert McCarty did not escape his share of rough wallops, even though he was now domiciled in the mildest climate the prairie had to offer—Southern Alberta. He had hail, frost, drought and sand storms, sandwiched in between his bumper years, as did everyone else, and the disappointments were not always easy to take.

There was that year, for example, when he had a hundred acres on the home quarter all ready to cut—a stand that promised a yield of fifty or more bushels per acre, and which would be ready for the binder in a few days. A white cloud, bearing in from the west, made Albert anxious. White clouds, black edged like that, often meant hail.

It was hail. It came down as big as marbles. It pounded windows and roared on the roof of the summer kitchen. It was soon piled three inches deep all over the yard outside, with everything living going down before it.

Father watched from the back window, but his worry at the moment was not so much for his crop—it was finished in the first few minutes of the onslaught. But Roger was out in this, down in the back field cutting oats. He had two broncos in his four-horse outfit. They wouldn't like this hail on their heads and backs. Mother and all the family were worried. Perhaps Roger had seen the storm coming and had been able to get his horses unhitched and into some shelter. But what shelter was there? The stones were large enough to inflict physical harm on Roger himself, and with the team to handle, he could not desert them and crawl under the binder.

It was when the last white ball had bounced off the back stoop, and the sun was already coming out in bland good will, that they saw him coming down the road.

His four-horse team was intact, walking abreast, plodding stolidly homeward. Roger was coming behind them, lines in hand, apparently unhurt.

Father put on his coat and went to meet him. The air, with all this ice on the ground, was as chill as winter. Mother and the girls saw Father stop to talk with Roger for a minute, then he took the reins from his son's hands and Roger came on into the house.

This eldest son had never been one to make a fuss. He had been his father's right-hand-man since he was ten years old, walking the fields back there in Manitoba behind plow or harrow when he was so small he had to climb up on the manger to put a bridle on. He had known all the rigours of outdoor prairie life along with his elders. This was just another experience.

Soaked to the skin, the removal of his wet shirt showed his arms, white above the tan, pounded into red blotches.

"S'pose I'm like that all over," was Roger's comment, as he pulled off his water-filled boots. "I didn't like it on my head. That nearly got me down."

And with that brief observation he disappeared upstairs for dry clothes.

Later it was learned that the team had all but got away from him. He had seen the white cloud approaching, and sensed it was hail. He had just got the horses unhitched when the first stones struck. The team tried to bolt, and it had taken all his strength to hold them. They dragged him through the standing oats and among the stooks, heels ploughing through the soft loam, until they found they still had a master and gave up.

Happily, the storm only got this one field. It by-passed adjoining sections and proceeded in a narrow, straight line across a strip fifteen miles long, cutting down other crops and gardens in its wake but leaving Albert still a good stand on his other holdings.

Frost made for keen disappointment. A field might be standing yellow and ripe, golden with promise, but investigation would show the heads empty—chaff only. Wheat kernels had been killed by perhaps only a few moments of below-freezing temperature, and the crop was valueless.

But despite all the bad luck, reward always exceeded losses, and Albert's progress toward prosperity—even affluence—in the foothill province was continuous and certain.

A new line opened up to the ever-ready farmer.

There were not enough grain elevators in Nanton to handle the inrush of wheat which in a few years was pouring into the village each harvest. Range land was being so quickly converted to grain production—farmers by the thousands pouring in from the east and south—that provision for receiving Nature's bounty could not keep pace with requirements.

Albert learned it was possible to track buy. With connections established between himself and Winnipeg, or even Fort William, he could buy from the farmers in carload lots, shipping his purchases direct to Manitoba or the Great Lakes.

Middlemen had always been Albert's bugbear. They had all his life taken his produce and paid him what they liked for it, often making a fortune out of himself and fellow-farmers by their paper transactions. Albert believed he could be a middleman who would not only give the farmer a better deal but provide himself with profitable occupation after his summer's work was done.

Thus did Albert McCarty—he of the backwoods' education and the meagre experience—first become a "grain merchant." This beginning was to lead him in a few years to an elevator of his own at The Coast—something he had not dreamed would happen when he and Margo first experienced that flying trip to Vancouver a few years before.

And it was Margo herself who now had something to do with putting the terminus-elevator idea into Father's head. Nothing has been said in these chapters, to date, of Margo's arch enemy—inflammatory rheumatism; but it was her periodical addiction to this calamitous malady in Manitoba which had weighed greatly in the family's decision to move to a milder climate. In Alberta she might escape these terrible attacks which, the last time, had confined her to a pain-ridden bed for six weeks.

But Alberta had not broken the jinx. After a year which she and Rosalie had enjoyed in Alberta College, Edmonton, she had come home to fall victim to another attack of her life-long assailant; this session costing her a year in bed.

Thus it was, all things combining to set the McCartys on the move again, that the family remained in Alberta only until the spring of 1909. A few more incidents, however, experienced or observed in the foothill province, may be here recorded before the pioneers were again transported to new fields.

There was, for example, the pretty wedding which took place in the front room of the new home, in January, 1908. Ranceford, Rosalie's childhood sweetheart, doing well in his venture in Lacombe, was ready to claim his bride. A minister with whom both bride and groom had gone to college, Rev. Herbert Gordon, came down from the northern town to tie the knot; the local pastor assisting. In her beautiful white satin frock, roses trailing to her white shoe tips,

Rosalie and her girlhood sweetheart said their vows and became man and wife.

Then there were such incidents as that prairie fire, in which Father was a central figure. Although nothing calamitous happened, the episode gave him a taste of what might, and often did occur in the wide-open spaces of this new land.

The Pioneer had soon found that Alberta offered him a fine field in which to exercise his early-acquired ambition to be a preacher. Very little of this great province was served with ministers. Towns along the railway might have pastors of several denominations moving back and forth from one centre to another on alternate Sundays, but the great areas to the east and the west, forty, fifty or more miles from a town, had no churches.

Backed by the Nanton pastor, Father had established regular Sunday appointments in several of the outlying schoolhouses, visiting each one in turn once a month.

This late summer afternoon he was headed for Lone Hollow, far to the east of the town. It was windy and hot, but there were twenty or more smiling children waiting for him when he arrived. In this centre elders absolutely refused to drop their everyday duties long enough to come to church, so this congregation was made up entirely of ranch young folk.

Father noticed, as his session progressed, that it was growing dark, although still in mid-afternoon. There was unmistakable smoke in the air. That was not, in itself, alarming, as there had been many prairie fires lately, and the air was heavy with that fall tang of burning grass. It was not until the evidence grew more pronounced that he stepped down from the platform to look out of the window.

Then he saw it coming. A great wall of red-tinged smoke was rolling in from the south. Seeing the alarm in his face, the whole school was immediately on its feet, rushing to windows and door. In an instant there was bedlam; children crying, clinging to each other, and the two women teachers scarcely less frightened. A roaring prairie fire was sweeping toward them, travelling as fast as a horse could run. They were directly in its path, and there was no way of escape.

Albert immediately went out to look at the fireguard. Every building had a fireguard in this wind-swept prairie. Yes, there was a ten-foot strip of ploughing all around the school and sheds. He believed it would hold. He went to the stable, where he and the children had tied their horses. It was quite a big building, as Lone Hollow school served as a community centre for a large surrounding area, and community effort had provided accommodation for sixteen teams. Albert had heard the story of this stable. The first one, in the process of construction, had been caught in a cyclone and the lumber scattered far and wide over the prairie. The second had burned down; a prairie fire jumping the guard to set the haystack on fire. Now once again the structure was threatened.

As he opened the door, the horses whinnied pitifully. They had smelled the approaching fire and struggled to be free. None, as yet, had broken its rope, so Albert shut the door and went back to the school. It was so smoke-filled that breathing was difficult. Yet there was nothing to do but remain inside. Hysteria was everywhere in evidence, with the teachers helpless to still the bedlam.

Albert mounted the platform and pounded on the desk.

"Children," he called cheerily, "there is a good fireguard around us. We are going to be all right. And while we wait for the fire to go by we'll have a good sing."

And with one of the teachers persuaded to take her place at the organ Father whooped up one of his favourite songs in his loudest voice, with some of the children joining in.

All were allowed to rush to windows, however, to watch the stampede of terrified cattle that thundered through the school yard. Behind them came mother cows with their little calves in tow, the elder animals encouraging their weary offspring to greater effort.

It was all over in half an hour. The great wall of flame divided as it struck the school guard, and swept around them on both sides. Only the all-enveloping smoke, and the almost unbearable wave of heat which filled the school occasioned for a time real danger of suffocation.

Albert called to the children when things were at their worst to lie down on the floor. There the air was more bearable.

When the roar had died away beyond them, and the smoke was beginning to clear, Albert held a little thanksgiving service, in which there was timorous concurrence from the still frightened children. The stable had not been touched, but there was yet the matter of getting home through the blackened fields; and—would they find their homes standing when they got there?

It was an anxious day, both for parents and children. Some elders had struck out for the school when they saw the fire coming, but had been forced to take shelter en route in an oasis offered by some fire-guarded homesite. One mother, it was later learned, had had a very narrow escape. Confused and lost in the overwhelming smoke she had only been able to save herself and horse by getting into a deep trout pool in the little creek that wound its way through the flat lands.

Soon riders and a few wagons appeared at the school through the heavy pall; faces of drivers and riders alike blackened by the smudge which kicked up from the burned-over grass.

Haystacks had been lost, it was stated, and at least one homesite—that of Sleepy Cane—had gone up in smoke. Sleepy was always too lazy to provide himself with a decent fireguard. Now the neighbourhood would have to put on a bee and run him up some new buildings.

Children who were on foot and who set off on a run for home and parents before other transportation could be provided for them arrived covered in black smudge. Albert McCarty, himself, when finally back on his own doorstep, frightened Harriett by his blackened aspect.

"None of us were hurt," Albert parried when his wife upbraided him for getting himself into such a mess. Harriett did not hold with Albert's incurable ambition to go far afield to preach the gospel. Plenty of work to do near at hand, she always maintained.

Another near-tragedy before the family left Alberta was that involving Albert's aged mother.

She and Grandpa had been persuaded to set forth from their comfortable home in Sunnyside on what Grandpa called—

"One last trip on the heels of that venturesome son of ours."

James H., outwardly opposing his son's pioneering urge which had first taken him from safe old Ontario to Manitoba, then on to this unchartered wilderness of the West, Alberta, was before long again converted to the wisdom of Albert's move.

"Sure and it's the Lord that seems to have no end of land up his sleeve," was the grisled old man's admiring observation as he drove with Albert from one farm to another. "Back in Ireland we were tucked in so tight we hardly had room to turn over in bed. But look at this—!"

Grandma and Grandpa McCarty were now well along in their eighties, but still ready for any new enjoyment; hence Grandma went with her son on many of his drives from farm to farm, or elsewhere.

This day they were going out to the foothills, to Williams Coulee, where Albert was to look at a team for sale. They had to pass through one of the many gates which now closed the old trails. Some newcomers had simply fenced in their new holdings on all sides, regardless of whether long-used trails were thus cut off or not.

With new roads on section lines as yet only beginning to make their appearance ranchers living on land beyond the fences were thus in many cases completely cut off from town or other objectives.

Such action made for cut wires and neighbourhood quarrels. Wiser newcomers put homemade wire gates across the trails, permitting passage wherever possible over the old roads through their farms. Even these gates proved a great nuisance to the long privileged cattle men, but they had to learn by slow degrees that the freedom of the plains was gone.

It was while Albert was out shutting one of these gates after his team and buggy (with Grandma as passenger) had passed through that something scared the horses. It was Pete and Gerry he was driving; a team of broncos which he had believed was now well broken. They had given no trouble all summer.

But now their sudden jump jerked one of the long lines out of the driver's hands just as he was shoving the improvised gate-end into its wire loop.

"Whoa! Whoa!" yelled Albert, trying to hold them with his one line. Running with them, as they set out on a fast trot, he was able to swing them into a wide circle around him, himself running in an inner circle like a circus trainer, clinging fast to his one line.

The prairie here was relatively level, which was very fortunate for Grandma. She hung on to the seat with one hand and her bonnet with the other as the rig bounced crazily over badger holes or natural bumps and mounds.

Round and round they went, the horses never breaking into a run but moving fast enough to almost exhaust the panting Albert as he followed them from his smaller circle.

Finding they were still under control the team at length heeded their master's repeated commands to "Whoa boys— whoa there!" and slowed sufficiently to enable him to creep up on his one line and finally get his hand on Gerry's bridle.

He had been very careful not to cut their orbit too small so that they would cramp and upset the buggy, precipitating its precious occupant to earth and possible death.

Albert was really exhausted when once back in the driver's seat; but his concern was naturally all for his mother.

"Are you all right, Mother?" he wanted to know. "Are you able to drive home?"

Grandma was fussing around as if looking for something.

"I seem to have lost my bag," she complained. "It had my knitting in it. There was half a sock finished."

Albert roared with relief. His mother was still a good pioneer. Her backwoods' training was now standing her in good stead.

"You're a brick," Albert applauded, and fishing under the seat he brought forth the lost bag, keeping a tight hold on his reins the while.

"These western critters," he said, as he steered the sweating team back into the road and headed toward home, "guess it's right that you never can trust them."

Grandma would accept no assistance when alighting from the buggy when once they were safely back in their own yard. Grandpa was more disturbed.

Taking Grandma's hand as they finished telling him about the afternoon's adventure he looked long into her eyes.

"I wouldn't like to take you home in a box," he said in his droll Irish way. "I've had you too long."

If the McCartys thought they had trials in Alberta, their hard luck stories were to be outdone by a tale brought to their hearthside by a young man from Manitoba.

He was a college friend of Roger's. Drumming up a little wherewithal to help out on next year's expenses at Wesley he was acting as travelling salesman for an eastern firm, and as such had visited Nanton.

While waiting for his train he spent the evening with the near-by McCartys.

His story was one that Father pronounced "heart-warming." Yes, one might have very trying experiences on the prairie, but it took such tough knocks as Keith Weston related to bring to light the great-heartedness of the West.

The tale started out with another hail storm—one that quite outdid the McCarty experience.

The Westons had settled a mile out of the village of Elgin, Manitoba, thirty miles from Brandon. They had done well, seven children, including four boys, all working together to make the farm "go"; and their two farms of 320 acres each were yielding good and steady returns.

The boys were all husky, athletic young men, and the hockey team, the curling and skating rinks, lacrosse and baseball teams—even the village band which Elgin tradesmen had sponsored—claimed their active participation. Indeed, the McCarty family, listening to the story, sensed that the Westons well typified the good all-round Canadian settler of which the West was proud.

It was in the summer of 1907 that the first really hard knock was experienced. A hail storm, with stones the size of pigeon eggs, swept across the home farm, and within fifteen minutes nothing was left of the promising crop but a blackened field.

Every window on two sides of the house was broken; and despite the efforts of the entire family to exclude the stones by holding blankets and robes over the battered windows, the floors in front of each opening were piled with the white brickbats.

That fall the boys went out to work, helping on neighbouring farms to bring in a bit of cash to keep the home fires burning; and Father Weston went the rounds of village stores to express his regrets that he would not be able to meet his yearly accounts this autumn (every farmer ran yearly accounts in Manitoba). He was greeted everywhere by warm assurance that the village would "carry him" until next crop.

It was an open fall, and Mr. Weston was just getting ready to get at the fall ploughing when the second disaster hit.

The horses began to take sick, and die. Within two weeks there was only one horse left out of twelve.

Appeals to the government to assess the cause brought a veterinary professor, on his own, from Toronto University. Spinal meningitis, was his verdict. He had been giving lectures on this malady ever since he was a professor, he stated, but had never seen the disease in action. He set up his cot in the barn and slept there better to watch the workings of the plague.

Contaminated well water, he affixed as the cause, occasioned by the decomposition of some small animal—perhaps a gopher.

Having one's farm used as a laboratory to study a new malady was interesting, but it did not help the situation any from a practical point of view.

Mr. Weston decided there was nothing for him to do but sell out. This brought protests from neighbours. They did not want to lose the family. How could the hockey and lacrosse record be maintained with those four stalwarts removed from the teams? How could Dad and Mom Weston be spared from the Baptist church and all the other community activities in which they so energetically took part?

They were going to take up a collection that would tide the family over, a delegation announced. Father Weston put his foot down on that. He would have nothing to do with such a proposal.

When spring came, an auction sale on the farm of a neighbour who was quitting was announced. His horses were little more than a pile of bones, for he was a poor farmer, but the Westons thought that they might be able to fatten the poor creatures if once they got them in their good pasture. Sales at such auctions were all on the pay-in-the-fall basis.

However, the auctioneer seemed to ignore Mr. Weston's

bids. Father Weston early dropped out of the bidding with a bitter, "Our credit is no good."

It was rather late when he and his son Willis got back to the farm, having to wait the pleasure of a neighbour to bring them. There were horses in the back pasture. He could see them from the road. Then the home-coming farmer recognized them as the eight he had tried to buy at the sale.

He never found out who was his benefactor, but the horses were his and, ever wondering, he and the boys proceeded to put them into shape.

"But they really aren't much good to us," he had to admit, ruefully. "We've got no seed grain."

Then, one bright spring morning around 7:30 o'clock, his two sons were startled to see a procession of teams, wagons, seed drills, ploughs, and harrows bearing down on them from three directions. All the family came to stare aghast, for the cavalcade was turning in at their lane! There were thirty-two four-horse outfits in the procession.

Father Weston managed to find his voice.

"What's all this about?" he asked Bob Moffatt, who seemed to be the captain of this enterprise.

"We decided to give you a hand. We're going to put your crop in."

When they left that night, the entire half section had been sown to wheat, oats and barley, in their proper proportions. Next day they did the other half section.

Others came in mid-season to do the summer fallow, and as they year progressed and the crop grew fence-high, finally turning to golden maturity, the Westons watched and wondered. They could not harvest the field themselves. What was going to happen? Then, one day, from three points of the compass, again a cavalcade was converging on their corner. This time it was binders and wagons that made up the processions.

Father Weston met them at the gate. Bob Moffatt was in the lead again. The two men looked at each other, but neither spoke. There were tears in the eyes of Father Weston.

"I have never seen my father cry before—or since, for that matter," young Keith now related. "It got us all in the throat. So they just all trekked in through the gate and set to work. Before nightfall they had both farms in the stook.

"And after it was threshed, not one of them would take a bushel."

Albert McCarty's face was glowing.

"That is a fine story, lad. It makes a man proud to be a Canadian."

CHAPTER XIII

Bob, the Black Stallion

I t was during the last summer the family was in Alberta that a former acquaintance from Clinton, Manitoba, reappeared on the McCarty horizon. Roger came home with the story. While he was getting the mail at the village post office he heard someone mention the name of Dick Slater.

A cow puncher, typically dusty and untidy, his leather chaps streaked with sweat from his horse and black with the grime of much wear, was at the wicket.

He was naming over the list of "boys" out there on his ranch whose mail he was commissioned to bring home. "Dick Slater" was one of the names mentioned. Roger wondered if it just might be the Dick he had known at Clinton and later at Wesley College.

That brief conversation he had had with Dick in the hallway at Wesley just before the spring term closed now came to mind. Dick had asked him about Alberta.

"I hear wages are higher out there than in Manitoba," Dick had said.

"It depends on what kind of work you do, I believe," Roger had replied. "If you are just an ordinary farm hand you fare not much better than in this province. If you are a cow puncher you get more. If you can really ride—are good at that trade—then you are in the money."

Roger had noted Dick's frayed cuffs as they stood there

in their black gowns, books under arms, waiting for the classroom door to open.

"I will need all I can get hold of to put me through next year—the last one for both you and me," Dick had smiled. "Besides, I would like a bit left over to start off with after graduation."

Roger did not offer much encouragement. He figured Dick would not rate very high on an Alberta ranch.

"I think I could work my passage to the foothills on the diner," Dick was saying, more to himself than to Roger. Dick was one of the "steadies" in the college dining-room, three times a day proving himself a first class waiter. These boys who were putting themselves through had to do anything and everything that came their way.

Now Roger and his chance cowboy acquaintance (Slim West, of the Lazy-K ranch out in the foothills, the untidy cowboy proved to be) moved across the board sidewalk where Slim could more effectively reach that tin can at which his surplus tobacco juice was being expertly aimed.

Yes, this might just be the Dick Slater of Clinton district and of Wesley College. Roger probed further.

"Well, he's a kind o' parson, I guess," the cow hand admitted, pushing back his soiled felt hat and scratching a thatch of uncombed hair. "Leastwise, he goes away on Sundays all dressed up, and they say he's away preachin' someplace—in the schoolhouse down the creek, mostly, I believe. He's a parson in the making—I reckon that's what you'd call him; but most of the time he's just plain puncher like the rest of us—and a darn good one at that! You know him, son?"

"I believe he might be the Slater who did a pretty good job on a bronco back in our district. He had a flare for horses—I believe he used to read up on how to break and handle them"

The cowhand laughed uproariously.

"That was where the joke came in on us. First he was a

sky-pilot. That was bad enough. Next, he thought he was goin' to break horses out'n a book. Gosh!—how we liked that! We wuz all set for the top show of the summer—nothin' much else having happened around them parts all year—when he volunteered to try a hand on Bob, the big stallion—after we had all either got our necks well nigh broke or our fool heads just about kicked off.

"And the terrible part of it was he did it! Yes Sir, by gum—he gentled that rip-roarin', 1800-pounds of the orneriest, cussedest piece of horse flesh I ever run up agin'. Five hundred dollars he made out of that deal—with only a bit arm and a few bruises to show for it.

"I believe he thinks his religion had something to do with it—usin' kindness and soft words instead of the spur and quirt. He thinks we use too much of that sort of thing out here in the West. But we ain't ever found no other way. Either we've got to be boss of the critter or he's boss of us.

"Of course old Bob ain't all gentled yet. He busts out occasionally when you ain't expectin' it, or when he takes a dislike to his rider. But then what range hoss doesn't. They never is all guaranteed gentle. A sudden scare, or a bit of back memory and they is just plain hell-raisin' range horses agin.

"But the parson did a good enough job on him to get his money. Three hundred dollars old Cap Walsh, the boss, said he'd give anyone that would tame Bob good enough to get him into harness, or a saddle, and actin' half human. The bargain was that Bob had to be driven through Black Fraser's yard and back agin (Black was the one that wanted Bob shot), and the same trip made in the saddle. And by cracky! Dick was the one that did it!

"And when us boys saw this slip of a tenderfoot deliverin' the goods—after we had made such a joke of him—we jes nachally dug down in our jeans and brought up another couple of hundred to add to Cap's wad. He wanted the money to get married on, he told us in that soft voice of his, bashful like—hadn't anythin' to git his weddin' suit with, nor buy the girl a ring.

"Well, that kind o' touched us all—us havin' no girl of our own, away out here in this gal-forsaken place. Hope she's a nice 'un."

Roger was thoughtful.

"Perhaps I know her. If she's the one I know she's O.K."

The puncher was interested.

"They met at her father's farm—if she is the one I am thinking of—old Bill Smith. He was a lot tamer after Dick got through with him. Perhaps that is right in Slater's line—taming things. They were friends at Wesley, later—Dick and this Clinton girl. I never could quite figure out how much that friendship meant, but at the do's we had occasionally she and Dick just seemed naturally to drift together, not talking much, but just seeming to understand each other. Dick never had any money to take a girl out on, but I ran into them a couple of times, walking in the woods, hand in hand. Perhaps she is the one."

It was from Father that the family was to get a fuller story of Dick and his new-found role as bronco-buster.

Albert's propensity for speaking to everyone he encountered led him to get into a conversation with a ruddy-faced rancher as they waited at the bank wicket. He turned out to be Cap Walsh. Father promptly took him in tow and brought him home for supper.

It took a whole evening, first around the supper table and later out on the front verandah, for the willing "Cap" to tell all he knew about Dick Slater and Bob, the Big Black Stallion.

Bob had been born an outlaw. And the worst of it was he should have been a gentleman, for his parents were imported Percherons, black as shiny coal, and Bob had a pedigree which might have made any range cayuse green with envy.

Brought with his mother from Scotland when he was but a little shaver, Bob was purchased by Donald Clay, and accorded quarters on his expansive and well-appointed horse ranch befitting Bob's birth and prestige. Beauty of limb, symmetry of contour and general elegance made the young colt promise much as a future sire; and it was to raise the standard of the strain of horses in his neighbourhood that his future was dedicated.

But from the start Bob had his own ideas about his destiny. Perhaps it was because his young nostrils sniffed in the clear Alberta air the tang of freedom—the buoyant possibilities of unfenced fields, of limitless range—that he early rebelled at the confines of his private corral and pasture.

No fence could contain him. He went through everything the ranch hands could set up. Once loose, he was off over the hills like a streak of black light, headed for whatever companionship the range had to offer in the shape of horseflesh; and it took an endless amount of rounding up and cutting out to get him disentangled from the terrified band, whose only instinct, of course, was to run from a rider.

Bob's heels and teeth were already in evidence. If he could not get what he wanted peaceably, sharp young teeth and angry hoofs were brought into play without fear or favour.

Ike, his trainer, early lost patience and administered sound thrashings on young Bob's shiny sides and black back, or bitterly retaliating legs.

Bob was not six months old when his keeper grew thoroughly sick of him.

"It ain't a horse you got there," he complained caustically to old Donald, "It's a wild hyena. And I don't give a throw if his blood is as blue as ink, I've had enough of him. Give me ten prairie-bred outcasts in place of this spoiled, pampered, high-livered brat. If you take my advice you'll stick a brand on him and turn him loose with the range scrubs. Perhaps they can teach him a little manners."

In the end that was what was done. No horse of that period found loose on the range without a brand was safe from thieves—or lawful claiming, for that matter; so Bob was brought out to the branding pen, lassooed about the foot, thrown, and stamped on the left flank with the Circle-H of the Clay ranch.

Astonished, humiliated, outraged at being thrown to earth, Bob's incredulity mounted to the boiling point as he found himself the helpless victim of red hot irons. They burned through his soft black hair and into his tender flesh.

Never had he run so fast as when finally released from his tormenters. Never was he more certain in his colt mind as he stood smarting and suffering there on the hillside that all men were hateful; that they were indeed the enemies of the horse, and that from henceforth he would never regard them with anything but revengeful venom in his heart. Let them ever try to catch him again!

For three years no one tried to catch him. To all intents and purposes he was now just another range colt, growing a thick coating of hair to protect him from winter winds, shedding it in the summer to roam the hills and plains unfettered and free, defying man or beast to ever again cramp his style with halter or stall or interfere with his will to do as he pleased throughout the length and breadth of the Alberta prairies.

Bob, however, had one weakness. He had acquired it in civilization, and it was ultimately to prove his downfall. He loved oats. Because he was destined for better things, Bob from the first was fed tasty mashes, oats whole or ground; and he had early shown a preference for having his meal served in a nose-bag. No other animal could horn in on that dish, and the strap hanging over his head behind his ears enabled him to walk about as he munched his grain, getting the last kernel out of the bag's bottom.

The boss knew of this weakness, and had instructed Ike to hang Bob's nosebag on its accustomed gate-arm, always ready for him whenever he should choose to come back to the ranch.

It was not long before Bob's eagle eye, gazing at his former jail across a sloping valley, spotted the bag, hanging there on the gate. At first he came at night, when no one was around, and after knocking the bag from its moorings, succeeded in getting his eager nose into the canvas and extracting all its contents.

As months passed, he grew bolder, and came openly in daylight, always keeping an open eye to spy out any enemy who might be hanging about, hoping to trap him. Particularly in the cold weather did Bob's thoughts stray back to the Circle-H, and when the snow was deep he came every day for his feed of oats. Hay, he found, was also waiting for him. Yes, civilization had its advantages; but— beware! Bob was always on guard.

The "boss" liked to be on hand when Bob came home. The boys had instructions to let him know whenever they saw the prodigal returning.

His admiration for the statuesque beauty of the fast-developing stallion was that of one who knew and appreciated "points."

"If we hadn't had to put that mark on him he'd have knocked the spots off anything in the show ring," was one regretful remark which brought forth caustic comment from Ike, the ex-trainer:

"Sure—he'd knock more than the spots off any rival."

Another glowing appraisal from old Donald—"Ain't he a picture!" brought a dry rejoinder from Ike—"But what's the use of a picture if you can't frame it!"

Thus always were Bob's outstanding qualifications tagged with a "but." What would the critter amount to, anyway? He was already making himself an unbounded nuisance on the range. Circle-H men heard complaints from all quarters.

Bob, now fully grown, was boss of his domain. He domi-neered mares and geldings alike; and should an unwary stallion dare to trespass on his stamping ground such a day proved disastrous for the invader.

Bob's harem was inviolate, and a rival on the horizon was signal for quick and drastic action. Seldom did an intruder escape the crunch of his brutal teeth or the blow of his deadly heels.

It was when tragedy came to the Circle-H ranch that a change in Bob's fortunes took place. Donald Clay was fond of his cups. Too often did he come home very late from the village bar, and this time he did not come home at all. They found him next day, lying in the bottom of the ravine which skirted the foothill trail. His horses, with their harness half off and no sign of their light rig, came back to the ranch and gave the alarm. Donald was dead, his face still bloated from the previous night's indulgence with other "well-heeled" ranchers.

As a result of Clay's passing, the ranch was put up for sale, and in the transfer of land and chattels the one article which no one wanted proved to be Bob. Everyone knew his reputation. They could not be bothered with him.

Cap Walsh, himself a famous "buster" of a previous decade, thought it a crime that any horse should so buffalo the human species. Man was not made to be the subservient dupe of a temperamental stallion.

Some of his boys, too, were ready to try their hand on Bob.

"I like 'em tough," Red Gould, who had learned his trade on the Montana plains, had offered.

"If we can't bust him, we can kill him," was Slim West's pronouncement.

So it was that a deal was made with the new owner of the Circle-H, Bob changing hands for a disgracefully low figure.

The task of lassooing the outlaw stallion and getting him, prostrate on the ground, into a halter was not so impossible. With several expert ropers taking part even Bob hadn't much chance.

A heavy wagon was backed up to Bob's great hulk, and his halter made fast by a stout rope to the rear axle. Then he was loosed and allowed to scramble to his feet.

That fifteen-mile journey home to the Walsh ranch was an eventful one, both for Bob and the two hands who engineered the trip.

When the unwilling stallion found he could not break the rope by sitting down and sliding along behind the wagon, front feet braced against the pull and hind feet slithering through the dust and gravel, he decided to ride. Rearing up, he came down with both front pedal extremities inside the tail board of the wagon, and there he rode, walking on his hind legs and glaring at the two guffawing teamsters ahead. Seeing he was skinning his knees in his repeated vaults into the rear of the wagon, one of the men managed to get close enough to pull out the tail board, thus permitting Mr. Bob more easily to mount the wagon floor with his front feet whenever he wished; and he "wished" for much of the journey home.

Indeed, it was in this manner that Bob made his triumphal entry through the Walsh home gate.

The ranch hands came out to see.

"What you got there—a kangaroo?" someone asked.

The kangaroo was wet with sweat, and white froth dripped from his angry lips.

Mrs. Walsh came to the ranch house door. She was a woman well versed in horse-lore, having been an expert rider and roper herself, often travelling the round-up with Cap in their younger days before they settled here in the hills.

Now she was sceptical.

"I've seen many bad horses in my time, Cap, but I never saw one that looked as cantankerous as this. Hadn't you best shoot him on the spot? Might save funeral expenses for one of the boys."

But Bob was allowed to live. He was turned loose, first in the near-by pasture until he should become a bit acquainted with some of the Lazy-K band; but shortly he was set free to roam the hills again at will.

Here ranches were somewhat closer together, and there was more intermingling between bands. Soon Bob was proving a bigger nuisance on the range than ever. He ran the geldings off the map, and he was a terror to every rider and mount on whom his eagle eye chanced to light.

A horseman was to Bob the greatest pest on the plains, for did not these leather-legged, lariat-waving, gun-toting upstarts take his mares away from him?

Orders had been coming in from the eastern prairies for more wild horses. They were being bought up in Saskatchewan and Manitoba to be broken and trained for farm use—just as had been the Pinto of a previous chapter. They brought forty dollars or more in the mid-west, and their cost of production in Alberta had been next to nil.

Riders, therefore, were very busy just now cutting out desirable steeds for shipment east. This practice infuriated Bob.

Mounts, travelling beneath a puncher, learned to dread Bob's onslaughts as much as did their riders. A horse and rider half a mile away was signal for a mad rush from Bob, and at his approach the hapless mount marked for his vengeance would turn and flee, disregarding bridle or quirt, as if all evil incarnate were after him.

The mounted horse was never any match for the unhampered Bob, and the awful spectacle of his thunderous pursuit, eyes gleaming, nostrils distended, breath coming hot with promise of dire catastrophe, was fearful to behold. Inevitably he gained upon the pursued horse until he had reached out those iron-built teeth and taken a cruel bite out of flank, side or neck, even menacing the rider.

It was Black Fraser from the ranch ten miles down the creek who came to the Lazy-K to act as spokesman for the rest of the hillsmen.

An ultimatum was in his eye. He sought out Cap and told him briefly his story.

"That black bear-cat of yours," he began, "he's fit neither
to be classed with man or beast, but—call him what you
will, he's gone one too far. Today he took after me on my
little bay mare. We couldn't keep out of his reach. His hot
breath was on my thigh, and although I slashed him with
my quirt he never wavered. I spected it was one of my legs
he was after this time—bein' not out to hurt the mare; but
instead he reached for the seat of me pants, and what was
in them. He missed me by about three inches, but his
ghastly molars came down on the cantle of my saddle. He
bit a chunk clean out of it! If he'd a managed to reach me
I'd a been minus one ham right now.

"So I'm tellin' you, boss, we don't like trouble in the hills
here. You and me's been good neighbours for twelve years
and never had any trouble before. But me and the boys has
come to one conclusion: if you don't take that gallopin'
gander off the range we're jest nachally goin' to peck him
so full of lead that he'll be too heavy ever to rise agin."

The Lazy-K crew debated. It wasn't customary to let
mere horse flesh run the range. Bob just ought to be put in
his place! They were going to make on last and mighty
effort to see if they couldn't teach that stallion some
manners.

Cap was sympathetic—and sorrowful.

"We'll do something," he promised. "I see I got to, or I'll
lose all my friends."

To his men he said. "He started life in a stable. Perhaps
he can learn to like one again. If we can't tame him there,
he's got us beat."

What the boys went through before they had Bob down,
bound and gagged and finally between the four walls of his
newly-constructed, iron-clad stall made horse-history in
them thar hills. The cost in sweat, blood and profanity was
epoch-making, but the job was finally done.

Then they found they had to cut a hole in the wall
through which to feed and water him. No man durst enter

his stall, even to scatter his bedding. In six weeks he was a sorry sight, plastered from head to foot with his own manure, skin knocked off hind legs as they persistently tried to batter down imprisoning planks, and hair worn off sides that valiantly strove to push over unyielding walls.

Bob's wrath at this horrible imprisonment knew no bounds. He chewed his manger. He stood on it with his front feet and glared out of his high window. There they were—his band—just across the valley, feeding on the hillside—and he here helpless to reach them!

This was the Bob that Dick Slater discovered when he arrived at the Lazy-K ranch that 1908 spring day. A sad sight was the stallion—a caricature, Dick felt, of the dignified, proud horse he was meant to be.

Dick felt sorry for him.

"Like a lot of people," he soliloquized, as he and Cap stood looking at the dishevelled, disorderly Bob. "Bent on destroying himself and all those about him because he wants to run contrariwise to life instead of along with it."

Cap was in no mood for philosophy.

"The thing is he's got us licked," the ranch man said gloomily. "And it's the first time anything on this ranch has ever got us down before. I hate to shoot him. A lot of good horse flesh there."

Dick was thoughtful.

"I suppose it would sound presumptuous, Sir, to ask you to let me have a try at taming him."

Cap, who had earned his title by reason of years of captainship of successive round-ups and whose experience with horses and riders was wide, pushed back his hat and stared at the slim young man beside him.

"You?" he said, polite contempt in his voice. "You are green, aren't you."

Dick was very humble.

"I could only fail," he said. Then—"I should like to try. I like horses. After awhile, they get to like me—any I've handled. Bob must have a soft spot in his make-up some-place. The thing is to find it."

Cap was stumped.

"Well, lad, if you don't value your life very highly you're welcome to try. But I wouldn't want to see Canada lose a good up-and-coming parson for the sake of trying his religion out on an outcast outlaw like Bob. But"—seeing Dick was in earnest—"He's yours for experiment. Let's see what I've got in my pocket here." He pulled out a roll of bills and counted them. "Three hundred dollars in that wad—just brought it from the bank. It's yours if you can tame him."

"Yes, sir," getting more enthusiastic. "If you can get him into harness and drive him down through Black Fraser's yard and back again, and do the same thing in the saddle—and get yourself home all in one piece and needin' no serious repairs—the wad is yours!"

The boys heard about all this. They thought it was rich.

"Jes like a fool preacher."

"Never heard tell of such barefaced conceit." Such were the comments. The men hung around and waited, hoping the tenderfoot would at least come out of this alive.

For several days nothing happened, except in the evenings it was noted that young Slater seemed to be very busy with a book he was studying. Word got around that the book was one on horse training, and that Dick was going to tame Bob "out'n a book." The boys gleefully waited. The summer had been void of any outstanding excitement, and this pending drama looked like a break in a season of dullness.

Dick immediately took over the task of feeding Bob through his inglorious "porthole." He found that even the fork, or the stick on which he poked through the pail of water, came out bearing the marks of Bob's teeth.

Dick asked the boys a few questions about Bob. Did he have a soft spot—a weak spot, one might call it?

Yes, volunteered one of his defeated guardians. Bob's weak spot was oats. If anyone had been able to do anything with him at all it had been with oats. With his nosebag in hand, some of the boys had even succeeded in getting within handling distance of the outlaw. Bob hadn't had any oats since his imprisonment, although he had come regularly for his feed up to that time, just as he had done at the Circle-H ranch. Bet Bob was sure hungry for his nosebag!

This tip was Dick's clue to a beginning.

Dr. Gleanson's Veterinary Hand Book and System of Horse Training, which was the young trainer's guide in this undertaking, had nice trite illustrations and directions showing how to tie up the front foot. With the animal on three legs you were his master!

The only difficulty was that the book did not say how to get into the stall with a horse like Bob and follow such very plausible instructions. How to bell the cat was left to the ingenuity of the operator, to all appearances. Perhaps the answer lay in the nosebag. Dick hunted it up and brought it around for Bob to see. From a safe vantage point in the adjoining stall Dick held out the bag temptingly and talked in wheedling tones.

"Want some oats, Bob? Nice oats. Come and get it."

Bob immediately recognized the bag—his bag. He frowned (laid back his ears) then perked up one ear, then the other.

Gosh! How he would love a feed from that bag! No smoker deprived of his tobacco had a greater yearning for his pipe than did Bob for those oats at that moment. Oats might make this awful situation in which he was prisoner a little more bearable.

But no, he wasn't going to be hoodwinked into docility by a bag of oats! Instead, he made a rush at Dick, teeth bared.

The young trainer was not discouraged. For several days he repeated his advances, and each day Bob came a little closer to the bag. Then one evening, Mike, who had a bet on this operation, was astonished on entering the barn to find Bob greedily eating from the bag which Dick held outstretched from his protecting adjoining stall.

"Well, I'll be . . . !"

"Shush! Scram!" Dick admonished in a whisper. This weakening on Bob's part was not for other eyes to witness.

Then the day came when Dick was in the stall with him, feeding him at close range, and without disaster. He even hung the nosebag over the big head, in its prescribed position, waiting patiently until Bob had finished the last grain, then casually removing the bag and departing therewith, unhurried and unmolested.

It looked as though Dick had won his first round. The boys stopped laughing and waited.

Then for several days Dick was busy down in the blacksmith shop, old Si Hawkins, the blacksmith and harness man, with him. They were up to something, but no one could find out what.

They were soon to learn.

Dick invited mike to watch this.

Dick was walking into the stall every day now, bringing Bob his daily treat. The animal even whinnied a little and smiled with his ears as his new-found friend came in with his nosebag. At least this man didn't beat him.

Today something new was happening. The nosebag today was covered with a black cloth, pushed down in a clumsy roll around the top. Bob noticed the difference, but after a suspicious sniff he smelled the same good oats waiting him and forthwith dived in. As the animal munched, Dick drew the head-strap lightly up over Bob's ears, just as he had been doing for days.

Bob, his head and eyes half buried in the bag, did not see Dick's next move.

A quick jerk, and it was done! Dick had rolled the black hood up over the stallion's eyes and ears, and with a sudden pull had drawn the slipcord around its top tight enough about Bob's neck to hold it there.

Bob was now in his nosebag from nose to ears, totally blindfolded!

Blindfolding was not something Dick had learned from his eastern-printed book. That was purely a western prescription. He had seen what a quieting effect blindfolding had on wild horses when the boys tied their neck-kerchiefs over an animals' eyes before letting him out of the breaking chute.

Dick was not taking any chances with a mere handkerchief on Bob. He wanted him totally blind.

The effect on the big outlaw was what he had hoped for. Astonished at finding his sight suddenly gone, confused, more intent on shaking this beclouding obstruction from his head than anything else, Bob did not know that Dick, waiting his chance, was slipping a rope around one of his pawing feet, nor that he had buckled a strong surcingle about the animal's huge circumference.

The leather belt had a ring attached, suspended under Bob's belly, and through this Dick had little difficulty in slipping the free end of the rope. In an instant Bob's left front foot was jerked from the ground by a strong pull on the rope, and before he could resist the foot strap was buckled securely to the belly ring. Bob was now on three legs, just as the book advocated!

"Gosh!" gasped Dick's audience of one. "You've got him! By all the powers that be, he's yours!"

Admiration, delight, and sheer astonishment kept Mike grounded for a full minute. Then he dashed from the barn to fetch the boys.

He might win his bet yet! Out of Irish contrariness he had been for Dick, while all the other fellows were betting against him.

Half a dozen incredulous cowboys, eyes agog, were to stand and stare open mouthed as they watched Dick now calmly fetch a pail of water and proceed to scrub Bob with a sawed-off broom.

"It will take half a dozen pails," Dick was saying. "Perhaps you boys won't mind keeping me supplied. He's an inch deep in filth in spots."

Bob all this time was snorting and floundering about. His audience awakened to a mystery.

"Why doesn't he chew the bottom out of that nosebag and at least get his teeth into action against you?"

Dick smiled.

"He can't. He's muzzled," he said briefly.

Old Si, standing delightedly by, grinned appreciatively.

"You tell them, Si," Dick suggested, calmly splashing water down Bob's reeking flank and continuing to scrub vigorously.

"Well you see—Dick and me," Si explained, "we fooled him. We built a leather halter with a muzzle attached inside of that nosebag, and Dick has it strapped around his neck behind his ears. He can't even open his big mouth!"

The boys gulped. No, he hadn't learned that out of the book, Dick admitted. He and Si had to figure out some things themselves.

Standing on three feet, Bob could not even kick. His wild efforts in that direction brought him with a thud to his one front knee, and he had difficulty in scrambling back again on his free foot.

Before Dick had gone very far with his washing he rolled down the black hood and took it off.

"He ought to see who his master is—the book says so," Dick grinned.

He had already secured Bob with a short rope to the manger. Now he produced another long rope which he slipped through the manger rope-hole, quickly snapping its prepared end into a ring which hung down on a strap attached to Bob's muzzle.

Then he removed the neck rope, holding the new lead taut the while, and triumphantly backed away, keeping the muzzle rope tight enough, as he let it slide through his hands, to prevent Bob's head from suddenly lifting from the manger to direct murderous teeth in his direction. In a minute he had tied his muzzle rope to the rear corner post at the left of the stall, also making the foot rope secure at the same anchorage. Bob was now captive from a muzzle-fitted halter and also from a foot hold.

"Remote control," explained Dick, regarding his work with much satisfaction. "He'll be suspicious of me next time I come around and probably won't let me in the stall. From this vantage point I can hold his nose to the manger while I get to him—even shutting off his wind with that muzzle strap, if need be; and the foot rope further places him at my mercy—until we get to be friends."

"Sugar breakin', that's what I'd call it," came from Bud Burly, Cap's head buster. "If us boys took time for all that tomfoolery where'd we get off at."

That was Dick's beginning. Working under the protection of his "remote control" ropes, Dick went in and out of Bob's stall at will, taking him carrots and other delicacies, winning his favour and confidence with daily evidences of good will.

It was only a matter of time till he was able to harness and unharness him without protest, finally getting a saddle on him and buckled about his great girth.

Then the day came when Bob was led forth from the stall, albeit on three legs. He did not like this restricted mode of locomotion, but there was little he could do but snort ominously and grind his teeth in his muzzle; for Dick was taking no chances yet in leaving Bob's molars unsheathed.

A drive around the yard without a cart, until Bob was really tired, hobbling along on three legs; then it was between the shafts of the light gig for him, Dick, holding the foot rope in his hands along with the reins. Now the young driver released its tension (the belly buckle having already been unfastened) and Bob was again on four legs, ready for normal travel.

But there was nothing normal about Bob's performance. Finding himself again on all fours he started in immediately to buck. Dick had made sure the bucking straps that went over his back were sound, ready for such an emergency, and now they were put to the fullest test. With every leap the cart came off the ground and bounced in mid-air, with Dick hanging on to his seat for dear life and "his head like to snap off," as one of the bystanders put it.

But the determined driver was able to stay with the battle, the special bit in the new bridle keeping Bob from bolting. Shortly tiring of this Bob was steered out on to the open trail and the last the onlookers saw of him before he rounded the hill he was stepping out in a smooth, fast trot, making a handsome picture in demonstration of the well-trained roadster he might yet become.

One lesson followed another, until the day came when Dick drove him all the way to Black Fraser's ranch, through his yard, before the astonished gaze of all the Fraser family, and home again.

Dick felt very happy that night. Half of the bargain was completed. He was getting closer to that $300.

The second half of the deal all but proved tragic.

Dick was handling Bob now without his muzzle, and he and his protegé seemed on the best of terms. On the day he was to ride Bob, Dick stood at his head a moment, patting the arching neck before swinging himself into the saddle.

On a sudden impulse, Bob became playful. Before the startled eyes of Cap and his wife and several of the ranch boys, the big horse suddenly reached over and grabbed Dick by the arm. Squealing with mischief he lifted his young friend high off the ground, then dropped him as suddenly at his feet.

As if pleased at this sudden return of his own superiority, he reared, his huge feet coming down on either side of Dick's head, just grazing it.

Mrs. Walsh screamed. Cap and the boys stood for a moment transfixed. It looked like the end of the gallant little parson. But Bob had done his worst. As if to prove he was only playing he nibbled at Dick's coat sleeve, as much as to say—

"Get up now. I was only fooling."

The captain rushed in, dragging Dick to safety, his face purple with anger.

A heavy scantling lay on the ground nearby. In a moment the wrathful ranchman had seized the stout stick and had swung it full weight across Bob's aristocratic forehead. Blinders on his bridle had prevented Bob seeing the pending blow.

The big horse went down like a stone. He fell on the edge of a dry irrigation ditch, then, the earth giving way, he rolled, saddle and all, into the ditch, to lie there motionless.

"Glory be," shouted Mrs. Cap exultantly. She had never liked Bob. "Just wait till I get the shovel and we'll bury him right there," she commanded, starting off for the house on the run.

Before she could return Bob was on his feet, blinking stupidly, but otherwise undisturbed. Without concern, he scrambled out of the shallow trench and went calmly to eating grass.

By this time Dick was on his feet ruefully holding his arm in his well hand. Bob's teeth had gone deep, and the wound was bleeding profusely; but before anyone could stop him he had walked over to Bob and climbed aboard.

"You fool!" yelled the captain. "You can't ride him with one arm out of commission!"

But nothing happened. Either all fight had been knocked out of Bob by that stunning blow, or he was not in the mood for further capers. At any rate, he trotted off down the lane with all the docility of an old plough horse, to come back shortly looking half asleep, his rider pale, but smiling.

"But was I glad to see that young fellah climbin' down to solid ground!"

Captain Walsh, the centre of the little circle of McCarty's who had been following his vivid word picture of this foothill drama, knocked the ashes from his cigar. Sitting there on the be-pillared verandah, six pairs of interested eyes upon him, this big brawny stranger from the hills seemed the embodiment of the alert vigour and vitality that belonged to this most westernly prairie province. He was the right man to tell this story, and he had had a most appreciative audience.

He was finishing his rehearsal:

"If anything had happened to that young parson I'd sure of kicked myself—getting' him mixed up with a critter like Bob and him just a green tenderfoot only just out from the East.

"But he came through it O.K., and we couldn't help admirin' his pluck, even though he was foolhardy to have tackled the job.

"When he clim down off that renegade I grabbed onto him and pulled him out of Bob's reach. Didn't want any more unexpected stunts from Bob that day.

"'Here's your money," I says, "and the girl that's gettin' you is gettin' a real he-man.'

"The boys had heard about the girl, and before I knowd what they was doin' they was passin' the hat. Everyone had come out to see if Dick would get back safe, and the crew was all there. In about two jerks they had rounded up another two hundred bones for the parson and his girl.

"Dick just stood there, pale from his arm, but now paler still. He looked at that pile of dough, and he looked at us, and all he could gulp was—

"'So this is the West!'

"Thinkin' he was pretty close to blubbering I got hold of him and got him into the house. His arm was really hurt— not broke, so far as we could tell, but bruised right to the bone. It took weeks to be any good again!"

The captain had just one more picture to recall. It made him chuckle.

"I have a gelding—Old Buck, we call him. He was afflicted with that awful disease for which they ain't much cure—balkiness. But Bob cured him.

"Bob has got to be a real useful horse around the place. Once conquered, he seems to like being civilized. The boys have followed up Dick's lead, and whenever he gets rambunctious they tie up his foot. We have used him in the wagon on the road, and—to make him real humble—we have worked him on the plow.

"Well, it was when he was workin' with the four-horse tandem on the gang-plow that Old Buck, just ahead of him, took a notion to balk. He came back in his collar, right in Bob's face. Bob didn't waste a minute. He just reached out and sank his big teeth deep into Buck's flank!"

The captain roared.

"You should have seen Buck climb into his collar and heave ahead like he would break every trace and both lines That's been the last time Buck has tried that stunt! I can thank Bob for that."

Ross had foregone his usual evening at the ball field to hear the finish of the captain's story. Roger was sitting on the verandah floor, back to pillar, alternately puffing his pipe and chuckling at the rehearsal. Because Dick, a college mate, was the hero involved the story held special interest for him; but even Mother had let her dishes stand while this glimpse of foothill lore was being delivered.

Margo—wan pale, Margo, still convalescing from her recent illness—the illness they had hoped would not assail her in this new province—had glowed at every detail. This was the West she had come to see. This was the West she hoped still to know more intimately. Young Chris at her feet had scarcely taken his eyes off the narrator.

Now Roger was saying something.

"Did you ever learn what her name was—Dick's girl, I mean?"

The captain hesitated.

"I got a brief look at the name on the letter he gave me to mail. He said he was writing her about the $500, and how that it was all clear sailing for them, now. A kind of queer name—is there such a name as Kelsie?"

Roger removed his pipe long enough to grin broadly.

"So it is Kelsie!" he said. The idea seemed to give him much satisfaction. Roger was never one to waste words. Now his comment was: "Well, all I can say is that Dick is getting a grand little girl, and Kelsie is getting a real man. And wait till I tell this horse story to the boys in the dormitory. Some of them think theologues are sissies, you know."

CHAPTER XIV

The Pioneer Spins the
Wheel of Fortune

I t is difficult for one who has experienced a run of good
fortune over a long period of years to believe that his luck
could, almost overnight, go into reverse and result in
devastating calamity, and Albert McCarty, at the time of his
transfer to British Columbia, would not have credited a
prediction that the move was going to be, for him, disastrous.

True, his reverses in fortune were not to come immediately after his arrival in beautiful British Columbia, for his
usual upward trend was to continue for some years. It was
when the depression preceding the 1914–1918 war hit
Canada that he, like thousands of others, was to feel the
impact of the tidal wave of lack which was to overflow all
America, and which, along with other factors, was to prove
his downfall.

When he arrived in Vancouver in 1909, British Columbia,
like Alberta, was experiencing a boom. People were making
fortunes overnight in real estate, on the stock market, and
by various other and often dubious methods. Lots were
changing hands overnight at ridiculous margins of profit,
doubling in value in the space of a few short months.

As an example of the hysteria, the fishing townsite of
Steveston, twelve miles from Vancouver, appropriated to
itself large areas of surrounding farm lands for subdivision

into town lots, selling most of these new "homesites" at astonishing prices before the crash came, and the wind went out of the bag. Steveston believed that it was going to be the front door of Vancouver. It was exciting while it lasted, but such an abnormal state of affairs produced such scandals as the Dominion Trust Co. steal, and many similar deceptions.

Albert did not get mixed up in real estate deals. He had put all his spare money into his grain elevator, and it took all available capital to get his business started and finance purchase of stocks. He tried to get on the water-front, where he envisioned himself as an exporter to foreign lands, but he was to find that critics of the C.P.R. had been figuratively right in their declaration that "The C.P.R. owned half of Canada." He found it either impossible to purchase water-front lots at all, or their price was fabulous and quite beyond his capabilities.

"Looks as though they don't want to haul any grain in this direction for export," was the pioneer wheat man's conclusion.

Father had to settle for a site on the great Northern Railway, near Main Street (then Westminster Avenue), and hope that this location would prove satisfactory despite switching charges and lack of waterfront.

The McCarty Grain Company did a fine business right from the start, however. There were still plenty of horses in the city as well as the country; automobiles being, as yet, the exception in transportation rather than the rule. The time had not yet come when horses were so rare on the roads that "the only time a horse gets scared now is when it meets another horse."

There were ever-growing herds of dairy cattle just outside the city limits, on Lulu Island, and elsewhere up "The Valley," and such farm stock, along with the great number of horses used in logging operations, made a ready market for Albert's feeds and grains. With competent office help and capable warehouse men, Albert was able to establish himself in those first few years in a very promising business.

It was not until the boom began to wane, and cash became scarcer, that Albert had any real trouble. Then customers began asking for credit, and who was Albert McCarty to refuse? Neighbours he had known back on the prairie had always been men of their word. If a man was in a tight spot, that was the time when he needed a little help. Here, he could not be hard, despite advice that B.C. was not the prairie.

Thus, Albert's soft heart proved an easy mark for the thin edge of future trouble. Things soon were decidedly tough. There was not enough cash coming in with which to carry on comfortably, and the business had to resort to bank loans for "temporary relief," with the comfortable new home up in Mount Pleasant one day finding itself mortgaged to meet an emergency bill.

This brought Albert up with a jerk. He must have more capital.

Roger had finished college and was now in a law office on Granville Street. Ross, the second son, had completed his course at Alberta College and had gone to The States pursuing a calling of his own. Rosalie was happily married and sharing a home with Ranceford in a northern Alberta town. Chris was in public school. Margo was in newspaper work in Calgary, having recovered sufficiently to attempt the fulfilment of a long-cherished ambition.

Father was glad he did not have three of them at school at once as formerly, but even with this cut in educational costs he was not making ends meet.

He had an idea. He had never quite gotten over his yen for the prairies. He was still a farmer at heart. Grain prices were good. He would round up twenty or more of those horses which the loggers were willing to give him in payment of their overdue accounts, and he would go back to the prairie for a year or two and clean up enough to get him on solid ground again.

He had a good man in the office. Reg Bailey had been a bank clerk, and knew all the answers. It had only been through a misunderstanding, Father told himself, that Reg had been let out of the bank. Anyway, if he had ever done anything wrong he was through and done with that now, for he had been converted in Dad's mission and was now a saved man.

Yes, Albert was at last realizing the desire of his heart. Night after night found him in down-town Vancouver, labouring among the unfortunate and down-fallen, leading the wayward back to legitimate paths. Working for the Lord in his spare hours made Albert forget his worries and kept him from regretting that he had ever come to Vancouver.

As an employee in the elevator Reg had proved invaluable. He could whisk the weekly accounts into shape in half the time it had taken the previous bookkeeper, and he had a pleasant way with him that often extracted payment for shaky accounts which even Dad could not collect.

After two years with the McCarty Co. Reg Bailey was practically manager.

So—thus it was that a reluctant and protesting Harriett, plus Chris, and a carload of horses, went back to northern Alberta to try to bolster failing fortunes.

The first year there was a frost, and Albert's beautiful section of tall, waving grain was in one night reduced to a field of hollow chaff.

No matter; next year would do it.

That year it was hail, along with a cyclone that took the roof off the house and levelled another promising section of nearly-ripe grain to the earth.

Albert gave up then. Guess Mother had been right. One should never go backwards, and in returning to the prairie he had been taking a retrograde step.

There had been unfavourable reports from the elevator, too. Reg seemed always in financial difficulties. The plant seemed to be slipping more and more, and there was even a rumour reaching Albert that Reg was not playing the game.

Gambling was rife in Vancouver. A returning relative warned Father McCarty that he should keep an eye on Reg.

The result was a return to the Coast, with Albert more bent, greyer, more tired looking, back in the plant office trying to pick up old threads.

There seemed to be no cash in the bank. There were a lot of unpaid bills. Albert was really worried.

It was the second night after his return from the prairie that the truth came out. It came out the hard way. Dad, beginning to wonder after his return from the office if he had locked the emergency door at the rear, went down to see.

There was a dim light in the office as he drew up at the door. Entering, a man leapt back from the safe. It was wide open. Dad switched on the light. Before him stood Reg Bailey.

"Why Reg," Dad said, trying to be casual. "Did you forget something? Why don't you turn the light on?"

Reg was in full charge of the office, and there was nothing amiss in his coming back to deposit some forgotten papers, or recount the cash, or catch up on his work by spending an evening there at the books. It was the dark room and the very evident confusion of the man that made Dad go weak at the knees and sick at heart.

Reg tried to stammer out a reply.

Dad closed the outer door behind him, and walked across the room. He stood facing the man whom he had trusted with his affairs—the man that wanted only a second chance.

In the bright light Reg's face appeared bloated with drink. He was plainly intoxicated.

"Well, Reg?" Dad spoke quietly. Reg opened his hand. A roll of bills fell out and fluttered to the floor.

"What were you going to do with them, Reg?" Dad inquired.

The quivering man, well groomed, well educated, from a good family, broke into tears. He sank into a chair and sobbed.

Finally, the storm spent, he spoke rationally.

"I'm glad you're home, McCarty. I'm glad you caught me red-handed. It's finished now. These months of hell are over. Do with me as you see fit. I'll take whatever is coming to me."

The whole story was learned. Reg had been caught in the gambling craze for which Vancouver, if not all the West, was noted. At first he had merely borrowed a few dollars a night from the elevator safe. If he did not win that night he knew his luck would change the next. The amounts taken became larger. His losses mounted. Always his change of fortune was just around the corner. He had no desire to hurt Albert McCarty. Albert had been his friend—had given him a chance when he was down and out. He had meant no wrong. It was just that the cards had been stacked against him.

Dad's face grew very grim as he listened.

"How bad is it, Reg?" he asked at length.

Reg hesitated.

"I'm afraid it's pretty bad. There are—a lot of bills unpaid. That's why I came here tonight. Things are so bad I felt I had to make one more desperate effort to right matters. I had to have cash to do it. I—have five hundred—or more—here—" He stooped and gathered up the scattered bills. He handed them to McCarty.

Dad was afraid to ask the next question.

"The grain—Reg—you aren't short on your grain, are you?"

There was a long silence, then Reg's tears started again, and all he could do was nod.

Dad leapt to his feet.

"You mean that you have gone that far—that you have sold me short—other people's grain that they trusted in storage to me?"

Reg's head was in his hands and he was blubbering like a great, weak child.

Dad turned pale with anger. It seemed for a moment that his big fist was going to shoot out and strike Reg down. Instead, he put his hand in his pocket and stood very still.

Caught with a grain shortage! And with no reserves to meet it! Albert felt a cold chill run through his great frame. But when his voice came, it was quiet.

"Give me your keys, Reg," he said. "I'll see you in the morning. I'm tired now."

Reg Bailey, for the second time in his life in deep disgrace, dropped his key ring on the desk and staggered out. Dad stood for a long time looking at nothing.

Then he took a turn around the plant. He paused to put his hand on the big grinder. That had been installed lately at great expense. He looked into the flour room. Stocks there seemed unusually low. He walked among the bales of hay. He stood gazing at the huge blower. All this—now burdened with a debt he knew he could not pay! All this brought to—shame!

That night the McCarty elevator burned down.

Next day Reg Bailey was discovered in his down-town room, a bullet in his head. "Suicide," said the coroner.

Elevator fires were common on the prairies. Sometimes the insurance companies were able to prove the work of incendiaries. (A fire was the quickest way to cover up a shortage of grain.) Sometimes proof was impossible. This case belonged to the latter category, but all suspicions pointed to Reg Bailey. A brakeman on a passing Great Northern freight had seen a man of Reg's description coming out of the emergency door at the rear of the plant in the early morning.

Further, the key to that door was found missing from the ring which Bailey had given McCarty.

Asked for his opinion of Reg's possible guilt of this final crime all Albert McCarty would say was:

"I don't know and I don't want to know."

He had trusted Reg and believed his reformation so genuine that disillusionment hurt too much even to be admitted. Anyway, if Reg had indeed been the incendiary, could not this final crime have been committed from a distorted sense of kindness—a "last throw" to save "the old man" from impossible debt and open disgrace?

That Reg should be more concerned over the welfare of his trusting "boss" than he was over a great injustice done an insurance company was small comfort to Albert, who believed in a square deal for everyone.

Charges against Bailey, however, were to remain unproven. Albert could help not at all at the hearing, although willing to establish justice. In his heart he simply did not know.

Eventually, the insurance company paid in full; and Albert found he had enough to meet all claims with a couple of thousand left over for himself—a fraction of what he had brought with him from the prairie.

"Well," said Father, looking ruefully at his depleted bank balance, "guess I'm the bum husbandman spoken of in the Bible—my talents have not increased—they've almost disappeared. But—we're not finished. The darkest hour is often just before the dawn."

To Mother's stormy denunciation of Albert's stewardship Father said little. Long experience had taught him that there were times when silence was the better part of valour. To himself he said, "I'm lucky this didn't happen earlier—not until I got the kids through school and on their own."

Albert's immediate need now was for a new business. The war of 1914–18 was in progress, and there was a greatly stepped-up demand for B.C. lumber.

This was a line of enterprise in which the prairie farmer had had absolutely no experience; and it was against the advice of a timber-cruising brother from Seattle and others that Albert turned his attention to this field.

Ross had returned home, and he and Father pored over figures, markets, costs and possible profits, and with prices what they were, it seemed they could not lose. Inexperienced they were, but there were foremen available who knew the ropes, and they—McCarty & Sons—could learn.

The result was that before the war had ended, Father and sons, along with a protesting Mother as cook for her immediate family, found themselves established in a comfortable camp on the shore of beautiful Narrows Arm.

At the end of the first year it seemed that all dire predictions about failure and disaster had been disproved. Booms were being put in the water at a satisfactory rate, and thus far all tows had safely landed through favourable seas to city harbours.

Albert McCarty would have succeeded, to all appearances, even in this field so foreign to his experience had it not been for that fire.

The summer had been extra dry, and everything was ripe for just such a calamity. A cigarette was blamed for the start of the holocaust, and high winds and continued drought were all that was needed to keep the relentless, devouring, calamitous blaze roaring through Albert's holding and on into neighbouring stands until another outstanding loss in British Columbia's timber wealth had been chalked up. Three months the fire burned, until the rains came.

For Albert, it spelled finis. It swept through standing trees. It roared over down timber. It devoured donkeys, cables—equipment of all denominations costing thousands. It belched into the camp itself, taking all sheds and outbuildings, including cook house and bunk house, even driving the horses down to the water's edge for sanctuary.

Everything went, except their personal dwelling, and that was saved only by the stolid refusal of Dad to let it burn.

Mother and the boys had fled to the beach. The smoke had grown too awful for further endurance; and anyway, the flames were right at their back door with sparks showering on the long, low frame cabin.

Missing Father, Ross, red of eye and black of face, came up the hill to look for him.

There he was, wet handkerchief tied over mouth, doggedly walking back and forth, back and forth, carrying pails of water from a near-by slough and sousing each new tongue of flame as it caught on the tinder dry roof.

Ross watched his father, wondering where he got his strength.

"Don't you ever get tired?" he asked at length.

Dad pulled the kerchief aside for a moment.

"Yes," he said briefly, and there was a humorous twist to his lips; "but I'd like a place to sleep tonight—and I want my supper!"

The kerchief went into place again, and Dad resumed his patient walk. Ross looked around for a pail, and soon he and Chris, who had arrived on the scene, were stolidly following in Dad's footsteps to and fro from pond to shack.

Before night fell they knew they had won. The wind had changed sufficiently to leave their cabin out of reach of flying sparks and debris.

The boys went back to the beach to seek refreshment in the cool waters of the inlet. Mother, who had been watching all this from the water's edge, now came slowly up the slope to pause before their now-safe home.

Dad, bleary eyed and exhausted, was sitting on a stump in the front yard. Husband and wife looked at each other silently. Each knew that this was the finish of their venture. Each knew that now, approaching their sixties, they were back where they started nearly forty years ago.

It was Father who finally spoke. Looking out over the smoke-curtained waters, he quoted: "A man's life consisteth not in the abundance of things which he possesseth."

Then, holding out his hand, he said, "Come Mother, let's go in and get some supper—and some sleep. Tomorrow we'll go back to town—and start over again."

It was well that Albert McCarty was Irish, not knowing when he was beaten. It was well he had faced blizzards, losses, setbacks, hardships all along the line, else he might not now have been able to gather himself together and go on.

It was not easy at fifty-nine to find work. But he must have it—anything—and immediately.

Ross had gone back to the States, promising to send aid as soon as possible. Roger had his wife and arriving family to care for. Margo had overshot her strength back there in Calgary, finding newspaper work fascinating, but strenuous, and had been forced to return to the Coast for a rest. She was recuperating on Lasqueti Island, some fifty miles away, having refused to come home until she could be a help, instead of a burden, to her mother.

Chris, now a husky boy of eighteen, looked for work daily, but without success. However, it was Chris who finally came to the rescue.

Father found him one day looking over an old truck in the back yard. It was a relic of elevator days, ancient, but still a truck.

"I believe it would run," Chris was saying, "if I could bum a couple of tires."

Father waited.

"I could deliver sawdust. You could take orders."

Sawdust at that time was fast becoming a favourite fuel in Vancouver. Formerly burned as waste at the mills, it had been conscripted during the war for stove and furnace use, and was proving increasingly popular.

That was the beginning of Albert McCarty's last business venture, one which shortly developed into a fleet of five trucks and made him, Chris and Mother a good living. Sawdust eventually developed into coal, and McCarty & Son, coal dealers, carried on this humble, but useful, calling until Father's final years.

And that those last years were now closing in on the old warrior Margo, in her island home, well knew. For that reason she valued and appreciated each new story that her failing father was able to recall for her waiting pages. She knew that soon—very soon now—he would breathe out his last Canadian tale, and the courageous voice would be forever stilled.

Conspicuous in his memoirs in these final weeks were stories of his mission and Sunday School experiences. Worldly prosperity had come and gone, gone and come. Father had enjoyed the battle, even with all its hard knocks. But making a living for him had been just a fascinating game, to be played with all the vim and vigour at his command—but it was still only a game.

The real things of life for him had always been his Sunday Schools, his preaching privileges, his mission work. Such pursuits had put the song in his heart that never could be quite silenced, the light on his face that never faded.

CHAPTER XV

Pacific Coast Adventures

B efore bringing to its conclusion the story of the Pioneer, a brief digression must here be made to recount an incident in the Narrows' Arm experience of the youngest McCarty, Chris.

Chris liked this most westerly province. For a prairie boy who had never known water deeper than Tobacco Creek, these wide bays, inlets, arms and gulfs were enthralling. Now nearing manhood, he had readily learned—since their move into Narrows' Arm—how to handle his father's gas boat, and he and his brother Ross alternated in captaining the *Dixie* to and from town, or about the inlet in which they now found themselves.

This beautiful stretch of water, almost cut off from the great wastes of sea lying outside, accessible only through the Scucum Chuck, proved an adequate playground in which the *Dixie* and captain might roam in safety. It was only when one must go outside that real care and seamanship were required.

For the Scucum Chuck was rated one of the most dangerous intakes all up and down this challenging coast. Four times a day a great body of water must rush through the narrow neck of the Chuck to fill, or empty the vast basin in the Arm, and many mariners there were who had lost their lives by challenging the Scucum Chuck at the wrong time.

Chris had never attempted to ride the narrows at full tide. Those who did get through when the mad rush was at its peak either had much more experience with such things than he, Chris reflected, or else they basked in special favour from the gods.

Father—land-lubber Father—had had a narrow squeak here. Determined to get to his Sunday School across the Arm one day when Chris and Ross both were otherwise engaged, Dad had taken the *Dixie* out by himself. All had gone well until the engine chose to fail when he was only a few miles above the Narrows. Only the intervention of two alert Natives on shore had saved him from being swept, *Dixie* and all, into that seething, swirling, mad tangle of froth and fury to his certain destruction.

The boys had bawled Dad out for that, and Dad agreed. Fast water offered a challenge about which he knew nothing, and he promised to keep clear of it in future—at least until he learned more about a gas boat!

This day Chris was on his way to Vancouver for supplies. Nearing the Chuck he could see the incoming water piled up ahead out there in the open, several feet above his own level. There was a lot of water to come in yet. He must be too early. He slowed his engine to a lazy beat and looked up his chart.

Rats! He had miscalculated by two hours. Nothing for it now but pull into shore and wait for the tide to turn.

A good landing beach waited him on the right. He had used it before. Today, even before he shut off the switch to glide like a silent waterfowl into the cool, green shadows of the little bay, he heard strange sounds.

A dog—evidently a little dog—was barking vociferously. Dogs made that kind of noise when they had a cougar treed, or were arguing from safe distance with a bear.

As his boat slid around the bend Chris saw it was neither a cougar nor a bear, but a man and a little fox terrier which centred this high shrill yapping.

A tall, lean woodsman, clad only in trunks and tanned a deep brown, was on one end of a long spinning log with the little dog on the other end. Both were running at full speed, their feet moving at a furious pace up the side of the log which was rolling, at an equally fast pace, toward them.

Chris grinned. He had already learned to "spin the log" back there at camp and he knew what fun these two were having. Every so often the pace got too fast for flying feet and dog and master were together, or singly, ejected into the water.

Then the two swam to meet each other and master put dog up on the log, and, each again in his place, the game started all over again.

It was not long until Chris and his in-gliding launch were discovered, and the frolic ceased. Man and dog settled gravely side-by-side on the log to wait till the *Dixie* was close at hand. The men exchanged brief salutations. Chris explained he was waiting for the tide.

"Me too," said the man on the log. He did not smile and Chris got the impression he wasn't very friendly.

"Looks like we've got to wait two hours," Chris ventured. "Had supper?"

The woodsman hadn't.

"I have sandwiches—and some other grub here. Think with a bit of coffee they'd go down all right."

The man on the log had been looking Chris over. Evidently he decided to like him, for he softened.

"I have a fire going on shore."

He slid off the log and into the green depths. The terrier followed and both swam to the beach. Chris followed in his dinghy. He found the fire and went to get wood.

"My name's Chris," he stated on his return.

The stranger was polishing himself vigorously with a towel.

"They call me Scout," he responded briefly. "The dog's Topsy. Come here, girl, till I warm you up." And he gave the little creature a brisk rubbing with his own towel.

"She's getting old," he explained. "She always shivers now when she comes out of the water."

Then he rolled her up in his coat and laid her gently by the fire. Evidently the little terrier meant a lot to this big woodsman.

Scout had bacon, and with provisions pooled the two had a satisfying supper. Topsy, also, was well taken care of.

Then Scout got out his rifle and set about cleaning it. It was while he was shoving the ramrod in and out that his grave face broke into a smile.

"There are some real saps in these woods," he remarked. Squinting down the barrel, he evidently found everything satisfactory, for he loaded the weapon, and setting the safety cock, laid the gun gently on the ground.

"Game wardens," he continued, reflectively. "We have to have 'em, but sometimes they're quite comical."

He pulled a sweater over his brown shoulders.

"Just finished meeting one like that on my way down."

Chris liked a story. He was sitting with his back to a tree, puffing a small pipe. He was criticized at home for this pipe; both parents holding that a boy of eighteen had no need for tobacco—Dad did not use it at all. Why should his sons?

This was just the atmosphere in which one could enjoy a smoke. He offered the woodsman encouragement, and soon he had Scout going back over his recent encounter with the government game warden.

It was evening and Scout was cooking his supper over a fire of glowing coals on the bank of the beautiful sheet of water known as Jervis Inlet. He had been hunting all day and had managed to bring down a mountain goat, and was now sniffing the savoury odour of goat steak as it frizzled appetizingly in the pan which he held over the hot coals.

His boat lay at anchor a short distance from shore, motionless in the still waters. The silent peaks rose up from the shadowy surface across the Inlet, still and quiet, and an atmosphere of peace pervaded the whole scene, filling the heart of Scout with content.

His steak was finished, and he was just about to commence the making of coffee when the bushes parted and a man unexpectedly appeared. Scout had not heard his approach. They eyed each other a moment; then:

"How do," said Scout.

"Good evening," said the stranger. "Smells good."

"Have some?" said Scout, with the spirit of hospitality common to the woods. Accepting with alacrity the stranger stepped into the open circle and was soon heartily enjoying the delicious meal.

They had little to say, but Scout was taking note of the visitor's every movement and manner of speech, and had him classified to his own satisfaction.

"Town bird," was Scout's verdict to himself, in spite of the fact that the stranger was dressed like a man of the woods and bore the tan of sun and wind.

When the meal was finished the two men rose, and Scout began packing up. The stranger cleared his throat.

"Well, now," he said briskly in a business-like tone; "you had better get your stuff together and come along with me."

Scout looked up questioningly. The stranger turned back his coat and displayed an official-looking badge. Scout recognized it as the badge of a provincial game warden. And goat was out of season!

The men looked at each other silently. Then Scout returned to his packing.

"You heard what I said?" the officer asked crisply. Scout finished his packing before replying.

"Which way are you going?" asked Scout.

"To town, of course," snapped the warden. "And you're coming with me. It's time you fellows learned that the law in this country can be enforced."

Scout considered this gravely. The stranger put his hand to his hip in a menacing gesture. The two men were about equal in size and the officer knew that his only superiority over his prisoner lay in his gun.

"How about my boat?" Scout asked.

"That's none of my business," the warden said harshly. "Step lively now, poacher, the night is coming on and we must be on our way."

Scout seemed to be indifferent. He considered the matter gravely.

"I really can't leave my boat," he said thoughtfully. The warden made a threatening movement.

"Will you come peaceably if I tow your boat down?"

"Yes." Scout began gathering up his belongings. "That's all right with me," he said; and in a few minutes he was aboard the officer's boat puffing out into deep water with his launch in tow.

The tide was coming up the Inlet and the going was laboured.

Scout knew it would take hours at this speed to get into open water, so he rolled himself in his blankets on the rear deck and went fast asleep.

Waking near daybreak he found the wind was blowing and out ahead in the open he could see the white caps rolling. At Baron's Camp near the mouth of the Inlet he found their boat was heading for shore.

"Too rough for him," Scout meditated, and getting the pike pole he proceeded to help the officer make a neat landing. The boats were safely anchored, and following his companion's invitation, he stepped into the dinghy along with him and the two men went ashore. They gathered sticks for a fire and prepared a breakfast of flapjacks, Scout officiating, neither man talking. The meal finished they paddled back to the boats and clambered in.

Scout was busying himself with the knot of the tow rope when his companion called out sharply:

"What are you doing?"

"I am untying my ship," Scout said gently, continuing to

loosen the hard knot. Proffering further information, he spoke in a very kind tone: "This is as far as I want to go, Officer. It was very kind of you to drag me all that long way against the tide. I was really a bit short of gas and this helps a lot."

The officer whipped out his gun and produced a pair of handcuffs.

"You put them on," he commanded. Scout took the handcuffs and laid them on the deck.

"All right, Officer," he said; "but just a minute." He was fumbling in an inside pocket while the warden stood tense and ready. Scout's search brought forth a crumpled and dirty piece of paper. Very deliberately he unfolded this and handed it to the officer. The other man took it and still keeping one eye on Scout read the soiled and blurred document.

It was a prospector's license which gave Scout the privilege of shooting game at any time of the year for his own use!

The warden read and re-read it. Then he let it drop on the deck and glared at Scout in mounting wrath.

"You . . . you," he began, his face growing purple; but he could get no further. Scout picked up his license, folded it up very neatly, then began pulling his launch in close so that he could go aboard. Turning has he climbed into his boat, he said, over his shoulder:

"I guess that you're a bit green at the game, Officer. Better luck to you with your next catch."

By this time Topsy had wriggled her way out of her coat-comforter and had crawled into Scout's lap. He reached for the coat, warm from Topsy's body, and put it on. The little dog snuggled under its overhanging warmth.

"Poor Tops," commiserated Scout, stroking her black, silken ears. "One of these days she won't be able to keep up with me any longer."

Then, thinking back—

"I lost her once. That was a bad three years for me. She'd never been away from me for more than a few weeks since she was a pup—just big enough to poke her nose out of my pocket."

Scout was off on another story.

Whether it was hunting, fishing, trapping, prospecting or ploughing the waves of the open sea, Topsy had been the constant companion of the big woodsman. She slept on his feet at night and shared good and bad luck alike with him. Small wonder it was then that Scout had a big heartache for many a day when he lost Topsy.

It was this way. Topsy was very reckless when aboard Scout's boat. She loved rough weather and liked to get out on its very stern and stand braced against the rocking and pitching of the waves.

It was when they were travelling along a lonesome stretch of coast line with the wind blowing in from the sea in no gentle manner that Scout first missed Topsy. He noticed that she had not been in to say hello with her cold nose in his hand for some time.

He was at the steering wheel in the cabin, busy enough meeting the big breakers squarely and fairly and still making headway on his course northward.

Missing Topsy, he whistled. She did not respond as usual; but as he could not leave the wheel he could do nothing about it. He was worried, but consoled himself into believing that perhaps she could not hear him above the din of engine, wind and wave.

There was no anchorage here, and it was hours before Scout was able to pull into a quiet bay and make search. Topsy was not on the boat. She had fallen overboard!

As the storm continued for several days, Scout was not able to go back over his course; there was little use when he did start forth again looking for Topsy. But, nevertheless, he followed back over the whole route of that stormy day, his engine running half-speed and his eyes on every foot of the shore line, on the possibility that his pet might have got safely to land. But no trace of her was to be found, and Scout was compelled to go on his way minus his much-loved little companion.

It was three years after that Scout was again following this rocky strip of coast that he fancied he saw a streak of white tearing across the beach to disappear in the woods.

"Topsy!" was the thought that flashed in his mind. Scarcely believing it possible, he nevertheless turned his boat shore-ward. It was calm and he had no difficulty in making a landing.

He went ashore and whistled and called, but no Topsy appeared. He found a place on the beach where something had been digging for clams, and the work looked suspiciously like Topsy's. He had taught her how to follow an air-hole down to find the clam and crack the shell with her teeth.

An hour of fruitless calling and waiting and of tramping about in the woods, failed to bring any other clue to light.

Scout tried strategy. He fetched some venison from the boat and laid it on the open beach—then returned to his launch and waited.

It was almost dark when the watcher was rewarded. A little white creature, thin and emaciated but unmistakably none other than Topsy, crept out of the shadows and ventured into the open to get the venison. Seizing it, she was off again like a streak of light, terrified of Scout's shouts to her.

All next day Scout tried in vain to secure his estranged little pet. But every effort failed. Three times she appeared, each time only to dash away again at Scout's first advance. She did not know him, and to her he was just something else to be afraid of.

That evening he fixed a trap for her. There was an old shack on the beach such as are common along lines of travel. Scout made sure that windows and doors were securely shut except one. Without a window pane, and high up from the ground, this opening suited Scout well for his purpose.

A long board had been washed up on the beach and Scout shoved this through the open window. Placing a tasty morsel of venison on the high end of the board, inside the shack, he set the trap at a nice balance so that any additional weight on the end inside the cabin would make it topple over into the shack.

Then he went back to his boat and waited.

It was almost dark when the little dog appeared on the beach; and she walked right into the captivity Scout had planned for her.

Following a trail of little pieces of meat which her would-be captor had dropped leading to the plank, the ravenous creature followed the morsels straight up the board. At the window she paused, afraid to go further: but the tempting supper on the tip of the plank was too much for her caution, and she made a final rush up the incline to secure the venison. The board tipped up with her weight and she fell into the cabin. The plank balanced back into its original position, and Topsy was trapped.

When Scout opened the house door to claim his prisoner a little volcano of snarls and growls greeted him. Topsy, accustomed to fight for her life in her three years in the woods, was not going to be caged and caught this way without a battle. She flew at the intruder, teeth bared and hair bristling. Scout backed out. He waited until her barks and snarls had subsided somewhat, then tried it again.

Stepping more gently into the room he closed the door and crouched on his heels.

"Topsy," he said.

The little animal was standing at bay in the corner, bristled for combat. This time she really heard his voice. Something in it brought back memories. Scout spoke to her again:

"Topsy, don't you know me?"

She dropped to the floor. All the fight went out of her tense muscles. Then inch by inch she came across the room, crouching, hesitating, with Scout still encouraging her, until finally she had reached his hand.

"Poor Topsy; good little Topsy," coaxed Scout.

"You're half starved and you need your old Scout to look after you. Come on, Topsy; come on home with me."

And in trembling surrender she finally crept into Scout's arms and snuggled her cold nose under his chin.

Scout was now on his feet, and the two began gathering up their few belongings. Scout pulled out an old silver watch.

"It will be just about right by the time we get there. Thanks for the sandwiches, lad."

In a minute he and Topsy were on their way to the beach, and, the fire having already been carefully taken care of, Chris followed.

"So long, boy," Scout called cheerily, as he stepped into his dinghy and made ready to paddle out to his boat.

"I always go through on this north side," he said, over his shoulder, as he moved out into the shadow-filled waters. "But don't let me advise you. Good luck, Chris. Perhaps we'll meet again some day."

Soon both boats were puffing out to the centre channel, headed for the now quiet narrows.

CHAPTER XVI

Harriett and
Her Little Ticket

꧁ ꧂

Needless to say, this panorama from the colourful past of the Pioneer was followed with keen interest by his wife, Harriett, who was now eighty-seven years old. Generally, Harriett approved of her husband's recollections, readily recalling time and circumstance depicted in each episode, but sometimes she would utter a sharp criticism because Albert had omitted some poignant incident or character. Once she complained that she, Harriett, was being left out of the narrative. She, too, had her memories.

Margo had always known that her mother had had a rough childhood, but it was not until this rainy day in December, with clouds hanging so low over Vancouver that they cut the mountains in half, and seemed to rest, like a heavy curtain on the very tree tops—with eaves dripping, making the interior of the comfortable old house all the more cheery—that Margo learned how really tragic had been the girlhood of this now-fading, snow-haired mother. She had been the Pioneer's valiant, if sometimes petulant, partner all through the ups and downs of their sixty-four years of wedded life.

For Harriett had not been the easiest wife in the world to get along with. Perhaps it was the suppressions and repressions of her youth that were to make her, in later years,

137

prove so sharp of tongue, so ready with censure, with her long, good-natured husband always getting the brunt of her eruptive moods.

Too hard, too harsh, had been those experiences which followed in the wake of her father's death, when Harriett was but seven. Too hard had been the lot of thousands of other children of that era, Margo well knew, when no child welfare organization, no mothers' or old age assistance was even thought of by either provincial or federal governments. Harriett's tale made evident that whatever deficiencies present-day governments might manifest, they had come a long way since those days of 1860 and thereafter, when over-tried individuals either battled it out alone or perished by the wayside.

Harriett's story started on a happy note. She was showing Margo some of her cherished scrapbooks. Mother seemed to have had a very good sense of news values, for national and personal highlights of a lifetime were chronicled in these voluminous books of pictures and clippings. Royalty predominated. Harriett had a great flair for kings and queens and little princesses. Family history was recorded in prose and picture, with lineage proudly traced back to that titled lady in her own family tree, of whom Harriett never ceased to be proud.

However, this day, it was something very small, and apparently very insignificant, that Mother was displaying to Margo.

"My little ticket," Harriett was saying, "This is what I got my pension on."

Harriett had been put on the books of that great family of old-age pensioners a few years before, and her delight at being a regular recipient of a whole fifty dollars a month, all her own, knew no shadow of hurt pride. The District Visitor had explained it so nicely:

"Not ten per cent of Canada's senior citizens were self-supporting when they reached the age of eighty," she elaborated. Scarcely more were able to meet their own requirements at seventy. Unexpected hard luck, illness, calls for assistance from the old folk for junior members of the family just getting started in life, and many other factors brought the best and thriftiest of Canadians to their final years without adequate security. Harriett had given her best to her country for eighty or more years. Now her country could do something for her! And Harriett found it much easier to accept sustenance from an impersonal government, which treated all oldsters in the same impartial manner, than to be under obligation to her children for benefactions.

The only difficulty about getting the pension for Harriett had been the little matter of establishing her age.

True, relatives were willing to swear that she was long past the required seventy, but that was not enough. Some record, to satisfy legal demands, must be found.

Margo wrote back to Harriett's home town in Ontario. No one at Walter's Falls could be found to verify her birth-date. Every possible avenue was tapped, but without success. No birth records had been kept in 1860, or for long years after, in that community, and it seemed that there was going to be a prolonged delay, if not defeat, in verifying Mother McCarty's age.

Then this little ticket turned up.

Mother had been very gracious to the District Visitor who came to see her from the Vancouver Pension Board, as she was to all callers. Mother sought to entertain her with the much-thumbed scrapbooks. The Visitor's eye chanced to light upon the Little Ticket. Partly printed, partly hand-written, the card read:

Methodist Church of Canada
Harriett Eleanor Caswell, Nov. 3, 1875.

"Why, this will do!" exclaimed the Visitor, apparently as delighted at establishing Harriett's claim as was Mother herself. And from that day Mother was "in."

"Where did you first get this card?" Margo now wanted to know.

That was the beginning of an afternoon's rehearsal which took Harriett back over an eighty-year vista, bringing to light fragments and facts with which Margo was to piece together a coherent story.

Margo had a sketchy knowledge of her mother's early background. She was the daughter of Henry Ackland Caswell, the village wagonmaker. Her early home had been normal and happy while her father had been able to pursue his chosen calling. Highly respected in the village and surrounding vicinity, being regarded as just a little above the average by reason of the fact that his mother had been Lady Ackland of Ireland before she migrated to the big house on the hill near Walter's Falls, Henry had made a good living for himself and family until relentless illness took him away in his late thirties.

Then began the struggle.

Sometimes in the old days a bereaved woman could fall back on a brother, an uncle, or other relative to gain aid in a time like this. But in Mother Caswell's home there was no one to whom she could turn. It was up to the young widow, not yet forty, to find some way herself to support her family and keep the little flock of four together.

Harriett's mother heroically rose to meet the challenge; but her best efforts were not enough. For two years she managed to keep the home intact with her spinning, her weaving, and even by washing—anything that would bring in a quarter, or—on affluent days—a dollar; but tragedy pitilessly and inevitably closed in upon her.

At last, her strength failing, her children lacking for sufficient food, with a fuel problem facing her in the coming winter that she could not meet, the unhappy woman was compelled to face her fate. She must give her children away!

No anguish of the human heart can exceed that of the separating of a mother from her young. Even today, Harriett recalls what unbearable grief that home-breaking occasioned.

The placing of Rebecca, the eldest daughter, now eleven, was not so tragic. She was merely to go down the street a couple of blocks to live with kindly old Mr. And Mrs. Simkins. They had no children of their own, and Rebecca was such a good girl they would gladly welcome her to their hearthside; and she could come home every weekend to see Mother.

Hector, the one boy of the family, fared much worse. Place with a farmer who promised much, Hector was worked far beyond his strength, and shortly instituted a series of run-aways that caused his mother untold sorrow; yet she could do nothing. Fate had given her this cross to bear, and she tried to keep her faith in the Almighty in the face of such odds.

Perhaps the hardest trial of all was parting with little Maggie. Margaret, the three-and-a-half year old darling of the family, black of eye and yellow of hair, was, to be sure, destined to have the finest home of all. Her parents-to-be were known to Harriett's mother, and they had long known and loved the Caswell baby. They would cherish her as their own.

Mother Caswell knew she should not so grieve as she crushed the little girl for the last time to her breast; and then and there she vowed she would never go to see Margaret, even though she was to live but nine miles away.

For a year thereafter mother courageously kept her vow. Then, one bright spring day the road over the hills seemed to beckon irresistibly.

"I should see how it fares with the child," she argued, knowing full well that in yielding she was only creating another Gethsemane for herself.

Over the long hills and down through the wide valleys she walked, all the rough nine miles, until the door of Maggie's new home was finally reached.

The child looked beautiful. Rosier, browner, healthier, better dressed indeed she was, with all the earmarks of love and care upon her. The weary woman was grateful, but—her heart now nearly burst with grief. Little Maggie did not know her! She had forgotten her own mother!

It was after the good woman had been fed and comforted as best the kindly couple could, and she had been sent on her homeward way, that little Maggie wanted to know:

"Why did that woman cry so hard? We gave her plenty of preserves."

It was Harriett's case, as well as that of her unfortunate brother, Hector, which was to prove how badly needed was child welfare provision in Canada, and how overdue were the protective measures brought in by federal and provincial governments in the century which followed.

"They have no children of their own. They will be kind to you," Mother Caswell tried to reassure her fearful little daughter as the child sat, bundle at feet and rag doll tightly clasped in her arms, waiting on the front porch for the arrival of her new guardians.

The Micks had been recommended to Mother as "good providers," and there was a guarantee that the child would be sent to school.

"You do everything they tell you and no harm will come to you—God willing!"

Harriett wondered if all were to be so fine as described why Mother must throw her apron over her head at this point and turn away to pace the verandah.

Harriett was only nine. Her big brown eyes were wide and plainly frightened when at last she was led down the flower-lined walk to the waiting buckboard.

She was not reassured by her first impression of the Micks. Black alpaca dress buttoned tightly to the chin, with grey-streaked hair drawn back severely to a meagre knot under her stiff sailor hat, Mrs. Mick did not seem to have any soft spot to recommend her. And Mr. Mick was worse. High cheek bones seemed to stand out above his ragged, drooping moustache, and his green eyes were sharp, without a single gleam of kindness.

Mrs. Mick managed to relax to affect real solicitude while still in Mother's presence.

"We will have strawberries for supper—and you may help me pick them," she chatted as Harriett was being helped into the wobbly old rig. "Then you can feed the ducks and chickens. You won't be lonesome."

Once tucked between the tall, angular pair, driving off with Mother standing there, trying to smile a brave good-bye, Harriett felt the atmosphere definitely change.

"That thing?" interrogated the bony man beside her, looking sharply at Harriett's nondescript doll. "Has it got to come along?"

"Let her have it," briefly advised the woman. "I had a doll once. It'll make her more content."

"She'd better be content!" came grimly from beneath the scraggly moustache. "She won't be worth her keep for years to come yet. She'd best know when she's lucky—getting a roof over her head at all."

Harriett endured the Micks for six weeks. She early learned that it was fatal to cry. That only meant a harsh scolding or a vigorous shake. Then there was always that riding whip hanging on the wall.

The day she arrived Mr. Mick had displayed its capabilities by deftly snipping off the tops of flowers and weeds at the back door before he took it into the house and carefully hung it on the wall beside the kitchen stove.

Harriett could not quite believe the whip was really intended for her, even though Mr. Mick had given her that strange, menacing look as he clipped off a dandelion head near her feet. There had never been any whips in Harriett's young life to date. She just couldn't believe there might be now.

Yet, in the weeks that followed, if there were tears, or other misdemeanours, her attention was always drawn to the whip. She dreamt about it at night, and cried softly there in the dark for her mother's protecting arms.

Mother had told her to do everything they bade her. She

never forgot that. That was the only way she could help Mother, she had been admonished. She tried to obey to the letter.

It was hard—dragging that heavy pail of water up from the spring behind Mrs. Sandall's house across the way; but then she could manage if she used both hands and walked very slowly. She learned to get it home without spilling much.

It was very hot in the corn patch, where she did the hand weeding while Mrs. Mick, silent and dogged, did the hoeing. In this new world it seemed there was nothing but work, work, with talkless meals and everyone "turning in" at the end of the day with but one thought—to go immediately into a heavy snore-filled unconsciousness that would provide renewed strength to put one through another day of endless toil.

Tilly, the rag doll, was a great comfort. She was always waiting for Harriett when the little girl climbed to her room at sundown; and Tilly clasped close in childish arms was a solace through the long nights.

It wasn't so bad when school opened in the log cabin down the hill. Here at least Harriett met other girls and boys and found that she could still laugh. It was encouraging, too, to have the teacher commend her as "a bright child," and applaud her when she spelled down that much larger Ezra Topp in the Friday afternoon matches.

But her schooling here was to prove of short duration.

It was just six weeks after her arrival that finis was written to her stay with the Micks.

It happened one evening when she had nearly finished her round of chores. The eggs had been gathered, the growing chicks fed their afternoon mash; corn had been scattered for the hens and water dishes cleaned and replenished. She had got down hay from the mow for Jenny, the horse, ready for her return with Mr. Mick from the field, and all the other duties had been performed as per schedule, except the feeding of the ducks.

Usually she gave them mash, but tonight Mrs. Mick brought her out a paper bag of dried peas.

"These is left over from the planting. I'm tired of seeing 'em around. Feed 'em to the ducks."

That was Mrs. Mick's order; and Harriett had just finished scattering the last handful when Mr. Mick rounded the corner of the barn.

The angular, unshaven man took one look, then made a dart toward the startled girl and seized the bag from her hand.

"You—you," he roared, red mounting his rough cheek. "Who told you to feed my prize seed to them ducks?"

Before Harriett had had time to reply he had seized her, his face turning purple with rage, and he was beating her unmercifully with a heavy cedar stick. He could not even delay to fetch the readied whip, but the blows that fell were quite as merciless as the dreaded whip could have dealt.

Terrified, indignant, flinching under each blow as the stick fell across hips and back, Harriett screamed for Mrs. Mick.

Mrs. Mick came to the door—and looked on. She realized what was happening, yet she raised not a finger. Although it was she, and not Harriett, who was the offender in this matter, she stood motionless while unmerited punishment was meted out to the little nine-year-old.

In going over it all through the long agonizing night that followed, when Harriett lay shivering between her covers, the little girl could not decide which had hurt the worst— the cruel stick, or Mrs. Mick's willingness to let her suffer unjustly.

Harriet had never known injustice. She had not believed such things would happen to little girls.

But, before morning, of one thing she was certain. She would run away. No sign was given at breakfast that anything untoward had occurred. Harriett appeared with her brown hair neatly brushed, braided into it two long plaits and tied with the piece of broken shoe string which Mrs. Mick had given her. She had carefully washed away all traces of tears in the granite basin on the back bench before entering the kitchen to set about laying the breakfast table, and no one gave any indication during the silent meal that this morning was any different to its predecessors.

Breakfast over, however, Harriett disappeared mysteriously upstairs, to come down shortly with all her meagre worldly possessions, including Tilly, tied in a grotesque bundle.

Mrs. Mick, drying the milk pail, spoke up sharply.

"And where do you think you are going?"

Harriett met the harsh eyes with as much courage as she could muster.

"Your mother's—Mrs. Kennedy. I am going to stay with her."

Mrs. Kennedy, Mrs. Mick's mother, lived just around the west hill, and she had been kind to Harriet. She had had her over for supper several times and was knitting a pair of winter stockings for her. She let her call her "Grandma."

"Huh!" snorted the hard-faced daughter. "You put those duds back in your room where they belong and I'll see John about this when he comes home."

"But I didn't wait for John," related the now eighty-seven-year-old Harriett, sitting here in her old rocker with Margo's eyes registering sympathetic indignation.

"I waited until Mrs. Mick had gone across the street to Mrs. Sandall's for water, and when she was safely behind the house, I took to my heels. I flew over the hill behind the house, dragging my bundle with me. I had to stop once because Tilly fell out and it took such a long time to get her stuffed back in again. But Mrs. Mick did not see me. She was talking to Mrs. Sandall—probably telling her what a bad girl I was.

"I got safely over the top of the hill and then plunged into the woods. I ran through the bushes for a long time, too scared to walk on the road. It was only when it goo too rough so that I couldn't go any further through the thickets that I used the trail. I knew which way to head, but I was not sure I could find my way. There were so many side-trails. I took some wrong turnings, and had to retrace my steps. That made the way so long. It was six miles, anyway, without any by-paths—a long way for a little girl of nine who had never attempted such a walk before, even with her mother.

"I would hear sounds on the trail behind me—a horseman coming, or a cart. I would be sure it was Mr. Mick after me. Then I would hide behind a stump or lie under some bushes until they had passed.

"Once I saw it was Mr. Finch on his big sorrel. He was going to the village, I knew, for he often went to the village. I had seen him there. I wanted to call to him and get him to ride me in front of him on his horse, but I was scared he could take me back to Mr. Mick's. So I walked it all by myself, although the day was so hot I got very, very tired.

"Once I heard people coming from the village way, and so I turned to the path beside the rail fence. That was all right until I ran right into Flannigan's big red bull. He was on the trail ahead of me, and he pawed the ground and shook his head when he saw me. I got out of there in a hurry."

Thus did memory recall in detail the incidents of that long, toilsome and fear-fraught runaway experienced by the little Harriett of four-score years ago. Margo pieced together the rest of the story.

It was late afternoon before a hot, tired, dusty little girl approached her mother's home. Mother was there, bending over her washtub on the back porch. Mother looked very tired. Harriett hated to let her know she had come back to be a burden. She stood on the walk, lips trembling, thinking it all out.

Then Mother looked up and saw her. The two gazed at each other without saying a word. In the big brown eyes of the little girl was a plea for forgiveness.

"I couldn't help it, Mummie," she faltered. "He whipped me. I runned away."

Mother came slowly down the steps and held out her arms. Harriett ran into them, and the two sank on the steps, sobbing together. Harriett had never heard Mother cry so hard.

No, Harriett would never be sent back there again. It didn't take long for Mother to reach that decision. Bruises and black marks on the little girl's back and legs turned tears to wrath, and made Mother's black eyes blaze.

"I'll deal with Mr. Mick!" she vociferated in tones that boded ill for the heartless offender.

But what could Mother do about it? What could she do about anything? There was no more to eat in the house now than when Harriett had been sent away. There was no future in the old home for a growing girl.

It was a Quaker couple, living in the nearby town of Meaford—Mr. and Mrs. Frederick Lake—to whom Harriett was next sent. Mother was sure her daughter would find only kindness there.

Perhaps the Lakes thought that they were very kind and generous. Perhaps they believed that they were doing very well to open their doors to a small stranger at all. Well off, with a large home, they had brought with them to Canada from England a great sense of "the fitness of things" to use a favourite phrase of Mrs. Lake's. In this case the fitness of things meant that the little household helper must know and keep her place. The kitchen was her portion, with all the tasks therein entailed.

Phoebe, the teen-aged daughter of the house, despising her mother's religious taboos, might sally forth clad in braid-trimmed velvet, with a real ostrich plume in her hat, but Harriett's wardrobe was based on grey flannel. Harriett was the household Cinderella, and, although Mrs. Lake essayed a great kindness to her, it was that of the lady for her maid, built on condescension and patronage.

"The hardest part of it," related Harriett, as the still-bright brown eyes looked dreamily down the long avenue of bygone years, "was to know that I was the grand-daughter of Lady Ackland, sleeping so peacefully over there on the hillside. Father always told us that we must never forget we were her descendants, and must try to live up to her. How could I, under these circumstances?"

It was at this point that the Little Ticket entered into the story. Harriett like church, and was a regular attendant at the Meaford Methodist Institution. Mrs. Lake granted her that privilege. It was when a good lady of the church, Mrs. Coward, saw fit to organize a young ladies' class, that difficulties were encountered. It was after the first session, which Harriett had enjoyed sincerely, that Mrs. Lake met her at the door on her return home.

"Where have you been?" she demanded, with much dignity. Harriett told her.

"We are just organizing. I am to get my membership ticket next Sunday," she volunteered hopefully.

"You'll do nothing of the kind," declared the Great Lady, "Once a day is enough church in that denomination. They just want to get another dollar out of you."

So Harriett never went again. She found it embarrassing to explain to the girls why she could not come, and she studiously avoided Mrs. Coward. However, the membership card was to pop up again many years after, in a most unexpected and remote place.

In the meantime Harriett continued to live her restricted life with the Lakes; at times inwardly rebellious and resentful, but knowing of no way in which she could better her lot. She was beginning to be called very pretty by the girls at school, and by the few young folk with whom she was allowed to associate. So she dreamed her dreams, and waited for the time when she could begin to live.

It was when she was fifteen that Mrs. Lake, one day, called her to the verandah, where she sat, fanning herself.

"Harriett," she said, "I have been thinking. You have been a good girl. I have talked to Mr. Lake, and we have agreed that if you stay with us until you are eighteen, we will give you a sewing machine."

Harriett, by this time, was showing an aptitude with her needle that made her ambitious to enter a dressmaking shop, when she should have the opportunity. A sewing machine would be a great acquisition. With it, she could earn her own living. With a sewing machine, she could gain her independence!

She thought it all out carefully, and next day agreed to make the bargain with the Lakes. True, she was working here for her board and clothes, but next year she was to have twenty-five cents a week spending money. Where could she better herself?

For three more long years Harriett served the Lakes faithfully and well. Always there was that reward waiting her, when she should come of age—that sewing machine. It would spell for her a new life.

Then came the day when Harriett was to get her machine. She had been apprenticed in Belle Armstrong's dressmaking shop for two years now, and pretty well knew such intricacies of the trade as the day demanded; for being a dressmaker in that period required craftsmanship of no mean order. Braden's truck brought the canvas-wrapped machine to their shop. Harriett could hardly wait for it to be set up and stripped of its covers.

When it emerged, a dead silence fell upon the room. It was an old model—almost an antique. It turned by hand, instead of with the new foot treadle. It was quite void of any of the new features which even at that time were considered essential.

Harriett felt her colour mounting. She had told the girls how long she had worked for this. She hated pity.

"Let's see if it will run," Belle briskly broke the silence. Anything to relieve that vibrant stillness.

She fetched a piece of white cotton and sat down. It took a long time to thread the needle. Finally the wheel was turning. Then—snap—bang! The thread had broken, and the cloth was bunching up under the needle.

"Let me try it," proffered Susan Crane. One after another, the girls valiantly wrestled with the stubborn antique.

Humiliation, chagrin, anger chased their way through Harriett's consciousness. She tried to laugh it off, but the laugh turned to a sob in her throat.

Then Belle was on her feet, her eyes ominous.

"I'll call Jimmie and he'll take it back to Mister Lake" (with sarcastic emphasis). "I'll tell him to dump it on his front lawn. The psalm-singing, saint-faced old hypocrite."

When Harriett got home, the sewing machine had been removed from its inglorious position on the front lawn, and carefully covered with a rug, on the back porch. Harriett found it there when she went to get her rubbers.

Yes, she was packing up. If only she could get out of the house without encountering either of them. If once the torrent within her were let loose, there was no telling what she would say.

Jimmie, Belle's handyman, again lent aid with his wheelbarrow. He was able to transport all of Harriett's meagre possessions in one trip out the front gate, down the street, and safely to Belle's boarding house, encountering no interference on the way. Mrs. Lake was standing at the foot of the stairs, when Harriett came down. She stepped forward to speak, but the look on her ward's face arrested her. She had never seen Harriett look that way before. It froze her into speechlessness, and all that she could do was gurgle some incoherent sound, as Harriett swept past her and out into the street.

That was the finish of another episode in the life of the Pioneer's wife.

And now—enter the Little Ticket again!

It was after the McCarty family had moved to Vancouver, that Mother decided, in 1912, to take another of her several trips back to see her mother in Walter's Falls. The aged woman was still living in the old house, married again, and once more widowed. But this time she had been left in comfort.

Harriett would go first to Jackson, Michigan, to see sister Margaret—now a doctor's wife with a happy home and a good husband. In the midst of their reunion chatter Margaret thought of something.

"You remember the Cowards of Meaford?" she asked. Harriett remembered. The mention of the name still brought a little shadow into her heart.

"Well, Mrs. Coward is gone—died two years ago. But Mr. Coward lives in the city here, and has a class in the Sunday School just around the corner. I believe that he would like to see you. He has mentioned you several times."

Thus it was that Harriett, thirty-seven years after her first contact with this former Ontarian churchman, again met Mr. Coward.

After the pleasantries attendant on meeting "someone from your home town," Mr. Coward said:

"Oh I believe I have something that belongs to you, Hattie. I found it among Mrs. Coward's little keepsakes. It is a membership ticket from the Meaford Methodist Church. Mrs. Coward never explained why you failed to get yours when the other girls did, but perhaps you would like it now."

The two sisters walked home with Mr. Coward and there secured the Little Ticket. It was brought back to Vancouver on Harriett's return home, and ultimately pasted in her most cherished scrapbook.

"And that is how I got my pension!" she concluded, triumphantly.

Margo's smile held no trace of derision as Mother, misty-eyed and a little tremulous of voice, added,

"God moves in a mysterious way, His wonders to perform."

CHAPTER XVII

The Pioneer
Reaches the Sunset

A s the shadows of his life's day lengthened, the thoughts of the Pioneer dwelt more frequently on the friends with whom he had worked, and the many whom he had helped, in Vancouver's downtown mission. They were the theme of the three last stories that he told his daughter.

A savoury chicken was bubbling on the stove in the kitchen of the comfortable home on Lulu Island.

"We're going to have chicken for dinner," Margo remarked to the convalescent Pioneer.

He smiled, and said:

"That reminds me. That's what little Freddie said—the day we had the celebration."

"It was at Wilson's Creek," he continued, drowsily, the picture slowly coming back to him.

"She had lost her purse. It contained her watch and two weeks' pay from her husband. Didn't she cry!"

He had gone to Wilson's Creek to start a Sunday School. That had been the life-long mission—or recreation, or whatever one would call it—of the Pioneer. Although work among adults who had gone astray and whom everyone else seemed to have discarded, was one of his favourite diversions (to use an unsympathetic term), it was among children that he believed he could do the greatest good. Giving youngsters some inkling of the hidden meaning of life, he believed, bore more fruit than voluminous exhortations after habits were all formed and sensibilities hardened.

He found a Sunday School already established at Wilson's Creek, with a discouraged superintendent labouriously trying to keep a handful of juveniles interested enough to come out with some degree of regularity to the Sunday morning assembly in the country schoolhouse.

Yes, the struggling leader had assured him, they would be very glad of any help that he could give.

As was his custom, the Pioneer spent a day in visiting. He found the population heterogeneous. There were the permanent residents, where the man of the house was a logger, or a fisherman, or a freighter, or a pensioner, or a farmer, where varying degrees of prosperity or poverty reigned.

There was plenty of the latter. Many were on relief. Many more were existing off the summer tourists who brought a little flow of money into the community for a few months each summer, and who fell for exorbitant prices from local gardens, because they could not do otherwise if they wished fresh supplies, and who paid plentifully for new-laid eggs or an occasional chicken.

Although the city play-folk grumbled over the "grasping" tactics of the year-round settlers, the latter seemed to have no option but to make hay while the sun shone. They must gather in these loose shekels while they were in local circulation, if they themselves wished to eat during the winter.

All of which has little to do with the story of the chicken and the lost purse. So, to get back to the starting point:

The Pioneer, now in his favourite role as evangelist and Sunday School teacher, found at Wilson Creek the usual B.C. coast population. On the summer tourist he spent little time, and they had little time for him. But the lonely settler, tucked in his cabin in the woods, half a dozen scarcely-clad youngsters running about; the isolated English woman of good breeding and surroundings, quartered in the small shack out on the point, wind-swept and isolated—these and many others welcomed his friendly smile, and promised to come out Sunday to "service."

Among such was Mrs. Hedlund. She was from Eastern Canada and had married the big Scandinavian woodsman, who was a "steady man," bringing his pay check home regularly and doing the best he could for the brood of four.

When the Pioneer located this cabin, set in a clearing well back from the wharf, he had little difficulty in extracting a promise from the boys that they would be on hand next Sunday. It was not so many years since Mrs. Hedlund had attended their own village church "back east," and she still had clothes good enough for church. So many hadn't. A print dress, patched and faded, a pair of greasy overalls, a fine poplin dress fifteen years out of date, these were what most of the women had as raiment; and a good many used such wardrobe deficiencies as their excuse for not attending church.

But the Hedlund family were among the score or more whom the Pioneer added to the attendance that first Sunday in the little log schoolhouse. They came regularly for three succeeding Sundays.

Then came the tragedy.

Freddie and Peter, the two little boys from the Hedlund home, met the Pioneer at the wharf. They were very grave.

"Ma can't come today," they informed him as soon as he stepped ashore. "She's lost her purse, and all her money; and she's crying like anything."

The Pioneer headed straight for her place.

It was as the boys had said. Floods of tears, bordering on hysteria, greeted the visitor.

"Nels told me to be so careful," was audible between sobs, "as he was giving me two weeks' pay this time because he wouldn't be back till then. And I've gone and lost it! And the kids needing boots for winter, and Nels working so hard. And—O it's just dreadful, dreadful."

This and more the Pioneer heard before he could get command of the situation.

"You all put on your hats and come to church," he recommended. "We're going to pray a bit over that purse; and I'm expecting you'll get it back. I've seen things like that happen before."

It took a deal of persuading, but finally, feeling she had nothing to lose, if not much to gain, the tearful woman followed her brood to the schoolhouse. Church service came before Sunday School, and before the first hymn was announced the Pioneer had explained it all to the sympathetic congregation.

Volunteers were called for among all who would pray for the return of the purse in the privacy of their own homes, while a little special prayer meeting preceded the regular morning session.

Some there were who thought this all quite a joke, chief of whom were the two nearly-grown Hedlund daughters. They had come reluctantly to church, chiefly to cheer their mother, and sat in the back seat together, sceptical and not a little cynical.

Mrs. Hedlund had told the Pioneer about them. Good girls they had been until those dances started at Roberts Creek. Not ordinary country hops they were, but Saturday night near-carousals when a boat load of questionables came up regularly from the city, bringing their own liquid cheer with them; and truly alarming were the tales that emerged about the goings-on of that "joint."

Mrs. Hedlund had pleaded in vain with her pretty daughters, but go to the dances they would, right or wrong, with the mother often walking all the lonely way through the woods at night to bring them home.

The purse episode had but climaxed a long period of nerve-wracking worry over her girls; and now this big man with the reassuring smile had herded them all into church, and was promising them a miracle. The girls were mildly grateful to the Pioneer in that he had at least stemmed their mother's tears for the time being, hence their acquiescence to his persuasion.

Next Sunday, as the holiday ship drew into the open bay at Wilson Creek, the Pioneer spotted two small figures in the boat which daily came out to meet the Vancouver vessel. There was no wharf at Wilson Creek, and the boatman usually came alone to take off passengers.

Today he already had two aboard, and they were waving excitedly, shouting incoherent announcements across the intervening water.

It was Freddie and Peter Hedlund. Shortly the Pioneer made out what they were saying—

"She's found it. She got it. And everything was in it. And you're to come to dinner. We're having chicken for dinner!"

This one-sided dialogue mildly interested the ship's passengers. They did not know what this was all about, but they had never seen a man get a more ardent welcome than was accorded the Pioneer when once he was in the boat.

Up in the Hedlund cabin a radiant woman awaited the trio. The Pioneer could scarcely recognize her as the same defeated victim of misfortune who had met him the previous Sunday

Her story made the Pioneer glow, too. Here was just about the best proof that prayer was some good that he had ever encountered.

"I went to bed and to sleep after you left Sunday last," rehearsed the glad woman. "And at three o'clock I had a dream. I saw that purse, just as plain as I see it now there on the table. It was lying just beyond a big log—that log you have to climb over this side of the trail. I knew it was the Lord telling me. I got up, and although it was still dark, and the ferns were just wringing wet with dew, I ran through them, getting sopped, and right to that log.

"There, just as I had seen, was my purse. It had fallen out of my straw handbag as I got over the log. There it was, and everything was in it—just as I dropped it—money, watch and all!"

The banquet that was served in celebration of this miracle was one for the Pioneer to remember.

The greatest miracle, however, was written in the faces of Sophie and Katie. The sneer had gone from their lips. Their eyes were friendly and frank. They were now ready to listen to the Pioneer.

The outcome of the whole episode was that Sophie became a teacher in the Sunday School. Katie took hold of the church organ and made a go of that.

The last the pioneer heard of them the Hedlunds were all moved to Vancouver, and he was invited to attend the ceremony by which the family en masse became members of the Baptist Church.

This time the tears in Mrs. Hedlund's eyes were those of happiness, as she took the Pioneer's big hand between her two.

"That was the greatest blessing that ever befell our family—losing that purse," she glowed.

"Yes, it's often that way," had been the Pioneer's rejoinder. "Seeming misfortune can be turned into good fortune."

The chicken on the stove still bubbled. The Pioneer sniffed it approvingly. From its aroma had emerged a pleasant memory.

The second story recalled by the Pioneer was that of his friend, old Mrs. Temple, known at the Mission as "Auntie," and the dauntless faith that carried her through what had promised to be a desolate Christmas.

Auntie and her invalid husband, whom she supported, lived in a tiny house in a lane off Cambie Street. She earned their living by gathering up washing from the neighbours; putting such laundry through her wooden tub, washboard method, and returning the clothes spotlessly clean to their respective households. During the depression, in the hungry thirties, Auntie found it pretty tough sledding to keep her little household in food and fuel, as, one by one, her customers had to inform her that they could no longer afford to have their washing done out.

It was a very cold winter for Vancouver, with much ice and snow, and one of Auntie's greatest problems was to keep enough fuel ahead to ensure warmth for her husband. He must not get cold, for then his rheumatic troubles multiplied.

It was the day before Christmas, and the day of her regular trip to the mission, that things looked blackest.

"We've got no wood for tomorrow, Papa," she confessed to her worried husband. "But I've still got one car ticket down to the mission."

"Seems to me you'd better forget about that mission this time. It's time somebody was looking after us, instead of you always looking after everyone else," protested her husband.

"I've always seen, if you do what you ought to do, things come out right," she returned, reassuringly.

It was in the afternoon that Auntie almost broke the commandment about envying. An East Indian man was driving past, atop a load of beautiful inside fir. His horses were plodding slowly but steadily up the slippery hill, right past her window. The load disappeared up the hill. The road was very icy. She hoped those poor horses would make it all right.

Then she heard a noise. The excited man was calling to his team, shouting incomprehensibles in his own language; and—there sliding backwards down the hill on Cambie was that load of wood, coming straight for her place!

One horse was on its side, and the other animal was being dragged backwards with the heavy load. Foot by foot they slid, veering more and more toward her ditch. Then the hind wheel was in it and the load had upset. Neatly it deposited the whole cargo right on her boulevard!

The driver was almost in tears. He had had many troubles that day. This was the climax.

Auntie was quick to accept this situation as the answer to her prayer. She hurried out to the distraught driver.

"I'll take it, Mister. Leave it right there. I'll pay you after Christmas."

The man was swearing unknown oaths.

"Broken axle—horse lame" (the animal had struggled to its feet). "All bad—all very bad. You take him lady—take him wood. I no can help."

"There!" triumphed Auntie as she ran back into the house to tell the good news. "A double load, and the very best. The Lord doesn't do things by halves. I've just time to bring in enough to keep you going tonight, then I must start for the mission."

But Auntie's good luck was not yet finished. Indeed, she ever after referred to this Christmas eve as her day of miracles.

She had just alighted in front of Water Street Mission, on Cordova Street, and was about to start the long climb up the dismal and dark stairs to the unlovely meeting place when a tall figure attracted her attention.

He was dressed in black, reminding her in some way of a preacher, but he was quite drunk. There was nothing noteworthy about that, but this man seemed bent on suicide. He was deliberately staggering into the street and right into the path of another oncoming car.

"Here," she yelled, and dashed after him.

She had only time to grasp him by one of his long thin arms and jerk him to safety before the car swept by.

"What you tryin' to do—kill yourself?" demanded the excited woman.

The tall inebriate stared at her blankly.

"Why not?" he asked in polite tones. "Why not?"

"You come with me," commanded Auntie, dragging him toward the mission door. "You need what we've got up here."

The tall man blinked dully and staggered after her up the long climb.

This was Miss Allison's mission. For twenty-four years Miss Allison had kept this hall open, sometimes having an audience of half a dozen, sometimes none at all. Her angular, ungainly walk made her a well known figure on Water Street, and her strident, shrill vocal efforts made her the joke of passersby when she held forth in street meetings. Her presentation of religion was not an attractive one. Yet through all these years she had had her successes. Many an old toper had lurched into her hall to walk out erect and with a new purpose in his heart. The Pioneer can tell many tales of interesting personalities who have passed through her bare, ugly meeting room from drunken uselessness to respectable living.

This man to Auntie was just another subject on which to work.

He slumped into the back seat as she finally succeeded in steering him into the hall. The faithful few were already gathered and were singing an old hymn. When they had finished the stranger demanded—

"Sing it again. I know that song."

Then he called for another, and another, asking for them by name. This man had obviously been to church before.

There were Christmas carols, these touching him to tears. "Silent Night," set him to sobbing.

With his head in his hands he wept softly to the accompaniment of the much-loved old carol.

And before the meeting had got well started he was at the altar, on his knees praying eloquently.

What a prayer! It was plain that this was no common Water Street drunk. Beautiful diction, fitting quotations from the Bible, were interwoven in rhetorical beauty as the man pleaded for forgiveness and asked to be received back "home."

Yes, he was drunk, and this might all be just the emotion therefrom which so many lost souls had likewise here before manifested, only to totter out into the night never to be seen or heard of again, or to reappear next night after their "conversion" in worse shape than ever.

Now this man was telling his story. Facing the increasing audience he told how he had been an ordained minister. After the loss of his wife he had taken to drink. His church had kicked him out. He was an outcast. He had been ready to end it all tonight when this kind sister had pulled him back from the path of the car. Now he was "saved," and nevermore could liquor tempt him.

Much rejoicing, and some scepticism, were occasioned by this Christmas Eve repentance, and the meeting proceeded.

Auntie Temple was so full of her own story that she did not pay too much heed to the stranger and his quick reformation. She had a song of thanksgiving herself to tell and when the hour for "experiences" came she was on her feet recounting the delivery of the load of wood to her doorstep, after all other means of procuring this necessity had failed.

She made them all laugh, as well as rejoice.

"It's no laughing matter," she assured them. "It's the direct work of the Lord. And now all I have to do is earn money to pay for it."

The tall stranger, by this time back at his place by the door, was on his feet again.

He strode toward her and dropped something in her lap.

"Why brother!" gasped the astonished woman. "You've made a mistake here. This is not a two dollar bill; it is a twenty!"

She hastened to return it.

"That's all right, Madam," assured the now evenly speaking convert. "I would have spent it at the corner saloon. It's yours—another gift from heaven."

Because there were many questionable characters in the room by now the Pioneer himself accompanied the affluent sister home. With a whole twenty dollars known to be in her possession Water Street was not exactly a comfortable place for a woman alone.

Old Basil's unalloyed delight was worth the trip to his place. The old man sat up in bed and laughed uproariously.

"Of all the women I ever knew, you do beat the Dutch!" he declared to his wife. "An' me tellin' you not to go down to that mission. By all the powers that be, I'll never advise her not to go anywhere and do anythin' that she takes it in her head to do. She's got a hunch for hunches, and her hunches is mostly right."

Nor was this quite all that befell the Temple household that cold Christmas. Regretful that they had had to turn their old washer lady away without her usual work just before Yuletide two of her customers had connived and had shared their Christmas luxuries with her. A basket on the table contained all that the old couple needed for a bountiful dinner, and there was a holly wreath to hang in the window.

Auntie's eyes were like stars.

"It's just the grandest kind of a world," she glowed. "And this is the grandest Christmas ever! I can just hear them singin' it—'Glory to God in the Highest, Glory to God!'"

The last story told by the Pioneer was that of the Ferguson family, and its triumphant conclusion more than atones for its sordid beginning. Jim Ferguson would, today, have been treated for alcoholism, but in those days he was repeatedly locked up for wife-beating. When sober he was a kind father and an excellent worker, but when alcohol reached his brain he became demented, and inevitably attacked his well-loved wife.

There were nine children, and all eleven were packed into a miserable shack on a side street in south Vancouver. Bobby, the eldest child, in particular, was the apple of his father's eye. He was fourteen when Margo first met him. He had come to the Pioneer's home to tell him that dad was "in again." He had a little brother by the hand—a youngster insufficiently clad and plainly in hand-me-down garments. Bobby himself registered poverty all over his ill-fitting exterior, but his face was what one remembered about him.

Sober to the point of gravity, the lad manifested a quiet patience that made him seem much older than he was. His solicitude for the little one at his side was very marked.

"He is like that with all the babies," the Pioneer had said. "He always has one of them on his knee, and he will share his last crumb with the baby. The baby is always his special charge."

The Pioneer did what he could for them when they were left without a father. For ten years this went on. The Pioneer, on more than one occasion, gave Jim up as hopeless. It was not until Bobby was almost full grown, and himself able to keep the family in necessities, that Jim's final reformation came. No one knew what happened, but this last trip to "the pen" seemed to cut deep enough into the inebriate's conscience to make his repentance genuine.

Albert McCarty had not heard of him since he had read of his last conviction in court, and he was surprised when one afternoon Jim, looking very fit and well, albeit humble, walked in the door of his office.

Jim's great anxiety this time was over his wife. She had told him never to come back. He wanted, above all things, to be reunited with his family. The kids would forgive and forget. They always did. But the wife. Did she really mean that she was through with him? Would the Pioneer go with him to find out?

As they neared the place, Jim's courage failed. A vacant lot next door was covered with willows and other brush, and into it he dived, pushing his benefactor toward the cottage.

"You must make her want me," he commanded.

Mrs. Ferguson's face lit up at the Pioneer's appearance. The children had already run to him and clung to him delightedly. He had a basket for them as usual; the woman at the corner store being always ready to throw a small hamper together when she saw him approaching.

"Have you heard from Jim?" was the wife's first question.

"Yes," admitted the Pioneer.

"Is he out?" demanded the long-abused wife eagerly.

"You'll find him—right over there—behind that tree."

No prodigal ever got a greater reception. Family ties— they were indeed strong in this simple Scottish home. They had survived everything.

Today the Fergusons have a nice little home of their own in Burnaby. All of the family of pretty girls and stout-hearted boys have turned out well. Mindful of their unhappy childhood, they have apparently made very sure that their courses were mapped differently.

Ferguson paid the Pioneer back every cent he had spent on him in those dark days, proving how genuine was his reformation.

One of Albert's most treasured possessions was a letter which he had received years ago from young Bobby. It accompanied a small Christmas gift, and Father showed it to Margo. Written in round, boyish hand was:

"You are the best friend I ever had, and I love you very much."

Then there came a day when the Pioneer heard a voice excitedly calling him in the street. It sounded something like that voice that years before had hailed him to tell of dad's latest conversion.

A handsome young man was pursuing him.

"Don't you know me? I'm Bobby. And this is Bobby junior."

A curious-eyed youngster was regarding the Pioneer blankly. A few words of explanation from his father brought a light of appreciation to the boy's face.

"Yes, he's heard about you, and how you helped us get out of the hole. I don't blame you for not recognizing me, but I'd know you anywhere. I'd know you among ten thousand."

So the Pioneer came to the Sunset, toward which he had been travelling all his valiant years. His monument is not raised in stone, but that of Albert McCarty, and the few others like him, is written all over the face of Canada. He "made land" in Ontario, in Manitoba, in Alberta and in British Columbia. Misfortune was but a challenge to him. He successfully reared five God-fearing children, but he was never too busy or too poor to extend a helping hand to the less fortunate. Like the friend of Christian in *Pilgrim's Progress*, he should have been named Evangelist since, wherever he found himself in life, he made opportunity to preach the gospel of simple goodness.

In death, he was not old. He had never been old, even though his departure came in his eighty-eighth year. His face, unlined—almost boyish—bore the stamp of peace and quiet rest.

To the funeral came a stalwart young man, bearing a bunch of violets. "May I?" he asked, indicating the flowers.

Margo looked again. It was Bobby Ferguson. She had not seen him since, a boy of fourteen, he had come to their home, seeking her father's aid. She took the flowers and laid them gently on the bier.

"He would like that—that you came," she said.

"I had to come. I saw it in the paper in Calgary. He was my friend, you know—the best friend I ever had."

"Thank you, thank you, Bobby," whispered Margo. "You have put into words what many hundreds could say of him— all the way from Ontario to Vancouver. You have spoken his epitaph—

"He was my friend'."